Independent Schools
Examinations Board

RELIGIOUS STUDIES
ISEB Revision Guide
(2nd Edition)

Michael Wilcockson

Independent Schools
Examinations Board

www.galorepark.co.uk

GALORE PARK

Published by ISEB Publications, an imprint of Galore Park Publications Ltd
19/21 Sayers Lane, Tenterden, Kent TN30 6BW
www.galorepark.co.uk

Design and typesetting Typetechnique

Illustrations by Gwyneth Williamson and Simon Tegg

Printed by Lego S.p.A., Italy

ISBN: 978 1 907047 70 1

First published 2011

Details of other ISEB Revision Guides for Common Entrance, examination
papers and Galore Park publications are available at www.galorepark.co.uk

Front cover photo: Detail from a stained glass window in Buckfast Abbey,
Buckfastleigh, Devon © Sharp/Alamy.

About the author

Michael Wilcockson was brought up in Cambridge and studied Theology at Balliol College, Oxford. After completing his PGCE at Pembroke College, Cambridge he was appointed Head of Divinity at Aldenham School and later at The Leys School, Cambridge. Since 1996 he has been Head of Divinity at Eton College. He was a Farmington Fellow at Harries Manchester College, Oxford in 2003 and Visiting Scholar at Pembroke College, Cambridge in 2010. He is a Chief Examiner for A Level Religious Studies for a large examination board and chief setter for Common Entrance Religious Studies for ISEB, as well as an author of many textbooks. He is a Fellow of the Chartered Institute of Educational Assessors.

Acknowledgements

I would like to thank the following people: Emma Wilcockson, Oliver Bullock, Alison Wilcockson, Nicholas Oulton and the Master and Fellows of Pembroke College, Cambridge.

Contents

Introduction

This revision guide covers Syllabus A of the Common Entrance Religious Studies examination. The chapters are set out to correspond to the layout of the examination paper. Chapter 1 sets out the key words and ideas that may be tested in Sections 1 and 2 of the paper.

Chapters 2 and 3 cover the Bible texts which may be tested in Sections 1 and 2 of the examination. They begin with Part a – short definition question; Part b – a summary of the Bible story; Part c – an interpretation of the Bible story and its ideas; Part d – evaluation of the story and/or contemporary ideas, for each of the Bible stories. Sample questions are given for each section and there is a Test Yourself section at the end of each chapter. You can use the Test Yourself answers at the back of the book to help you structure your answers.

Chapters 4–10 cover the 'World Religions and Contemporary Issues' section of the examination paper and provide a summary of the main ideas of each religion, with a Test Yourself section at the end of each chapter.

Good luck with your revision. Revision is never a very exciting activity, but if you do it well it can be quite satisfying and it might even mean you enjoy doing the examination itself! That, with luck, will help you get your place at senior school.

The syllabus and your exam

If you have *not* submitted coursework you have **60 minutes** to complete the examination. You must:

- Choose **one** question from **Section 1** (Interpreting the Old Testament) from a choice of four. Spend no more than **22 minutes** on this question.

- Choose **one** question from **Section 2** (Interpreting the New Testament) from a choice of four. Spend no more than **22 minutes** on this question.

- Choose **three** questions from **Section 3** (World Religions and Contemporary Issues) from a choice of 35. Spend no more than **5 minutes** per question in this section.

If you have submitted coursework you have **40 minutes** to complete Sections 1 and 2 of the examination.

Sections 1 and 2

There are **four** questions in Section 1 and **four** questions in Section 2 and you have to answer **one** question from each section.

In each section you will find the questions are placed in **two groups**. For each group of texts there are two questions. This means that when you come to revise, you can decide whether to revise one group of Bible stories or both groups for each section.

Clearly, if you revise the stories from both groups then you will have a greater range of questions from which to choose. On the other hand, you may wish to concentrate on one group per section and therefore know a smaller number of texts really well but have less choice in the exam itself.

Each question has **four parts** which become increasingly complex.

- **Part a** briefly tests factual knowledge or asks for a definition of a word or phrase.

- **Part b** tests factual knowledge of a biblical story.

- **Part c** tests your ability to interpret the story.

- **Part d** tests your ability to discuss and evaluate the story and often a contemporary issue raised by the text.

Section 3

There are **35** questions in Section 3. You have to answer **three** questions. Your teacher will have told you which religion or religions you have studied and therefore which questions you should attempt.

If you have submitted **coursework** to your senior school then there is no need to revise for this section.

(*Advice on coursework may be found on pages 204–205*)

Tips on revising

Get the best out of your brain

- Give your brain plenty of oxygen by **exercising**. You can revise more effectively if you feel fit and well.

- **Eat healthy** food while you are revising – your brain works better when you give it good fuel.

- **Think positively**. Give your brain positive messages so that it will want to study.

- **Keep calm**. If your brain is stressed it will not operate effectively.

- Take **regular breaks** during your study time.

- Get enough **sleep**. Your brain will carry on sorting out what you have revised while you sleep.

Get the most from your revision

- **Don't** work for hours without a break. Revise for 20–30 minutes, then take a five-minute break. Do a little revision often.

- Make a list of all the things you *don't understand* and revise these first.

- **Do** good things in your breaks: listen to your favourite music, eat healthy food, drink some water, do some exercise or juggle. **Don't** read a book, watch TV or play on the computer as it will conflict with what your brain is trying to learn.

- When you go back to your revision, **review** what you have just learnt.

- Regularly review the facts you have learnt.

- Look over your **class notes**, preps or homeworks. Make notes of ideas or themes that are important for each piece of work.

Get motivated

- Set yourself some **goals** and promise yourself a treat when the exams are over.

- Make the most of all the **expertise** and talent available to you at school and at home. If you don't understand something, ask your teacher to explain.

- Get **organised**. Find a quiet place to revise and make sure you have all the equipment you need.

- Use year and weekly **planners** to help you organise your time so that you revise all subjects equally. (Available for download from www.galorepark.co.uk)

- Use topic and subject **checklists** to help you keep on top of what you are revising. (Available for download from www.galorepark.co.uk)

Know what to expect in the exam

- Use past papers to familiarise yourself with the **format** of the exam. (Available from Galore Park)

- Make sure you understand the **language** examiners use.

Before the exam

- Have all your **equipment** and pens ready the night before.

- Make sure you are at your best by getting a good night's **sleep** before the exam. You will be able to approach the exam much more positively if you feel refreshed.

- Have a good **breakfast** in the morning.

- Take some **water** into the exam if you are allowed.

- Think **positively** and keep **calm**.

- Check that you have **everything you need** to take into the exam room. Take at least two pens in case one runs out.

During the exam

- Have a **watch** or clock on your desk. Work out how much time you need to allocate to each question and try to stick to it.

- Make sure you **read and understand** the instructions and rules on the front of the exam paper.

- Allow some time at the start to read and **consider** the questions carefully before writing anything.

- Read all the questions at least twice. **Don't rush** into answering before you have a chance to think about it.

- If a question is particularly hard **move on to the next one**. Go back to it if you have time at the end.

- **Check** your answers make sense if you have time at the end.

Tips for revising Religious Studies

- When using this revision guide, cover up the page and write down as many of the ideas as you can remember, *then* look again at the guide.

- Make sure you refer specifically to words in bold.

- Make sure you first learn all the key words which the examination board prescribes. These can be found in Chapter 1. They will help you develop your own technical vocabulary and provide you with examples of people and their ideas.

- Use the suggested 'for' and 'against' arguments to begin your own ideas. Make sure you make a note of your own thoughts so you can use these in the examination.

- Practice makes perfect so get your own copy of *Preparing for Common Entrance Religious Studies* (Michael Wilcockson). You could also contact Galore Park and purchase some past papers.

- For more tips on how to get the best from your revision and exams, see *Study Skills* by Elizabeth Holtom, published by Galore Park.

Useful resources

All available from Galore Park: www.galorepark.co.uk.

Preparing for Common Entrance Religious Studies by Michael Wilcockson,
ISBN: 9780903627603

Study Skills by Elizabeth Holtom, ISBN: 9781902984599

Other titles

Religious Studies for Common Entrance (second edition) by Susan Grenfell,
ISBN: 9780340887905

The Holy Bible (The recommended translation is New International Version but you
can use any translation you like.)

Seeking Religion: The Buddhist Experience by Mel Thompson, ISBN: 9780340747711

Seeking Religion: The Christian Experience by JF Aylett and Kevin O'Donnell,
ISBN: 9780340747681

Seeking Religion: The Jewish Experience by Liz Aylett and Kevin O'Donnell,
ISBN: 9780340747735

Seeking Religion: The Muslim Experience by JF Aylett and Kevin O'Donnell,
ISBN: 9780340747704

Seeking Religion: The Sikh Experience by Philip Emmett, ISBN: 9780340747728

Seeking Religion: The Hindu Experience by Liz Aylett and Kevin O'Donnell,
ISBN: 9780340747698

Chapter 1: Key words and ideas for Sections 1 and 2

This chapter lists the key words and ideas that may be tested in Sections 1 and 2 of the examination paper. Use the following list of words to test yourself. Cover up the right hand side of the page and see how much you can remember. These words are set by the examination board and can be tested in the short answer Part (a) questions.

LOOK, SAY, COVER, WRITE, CHECK

Ark of the Covenant	A sacred box containing the two tablets of the Law (the Ten Commandments).
Atonement	Getting back into a right relationship with God.
Baal	A Canaanite god.
Baptism	The symbolic washing away of sin.
Blasphemy	Speaking against God or making oneself equal to God.
Blessed	True happiness as given by God.
Christ or Messiah	The anointed one.
Covenant	An agreement between God and His people.
Crucifixion	The Roman death penalty of being nailed to a cross.
Disciple	A follower or student.
Discrimination	Acting negatively against someone or some people.
Eden	The garden in Genesis 2 where everything is perfect.
Exodus	A way out or departure from Egypt.
Faith	Having an active trust in someone or in God.
The Fall	The moment when Adam and Eve sinned and fell from grace.
Fasting	Going without food to enable oneself to be more aware of God.
Justice	Treating others fairly.
Miracle	An act of God which breaks the laws of physics.
Pacifist	A person who refuses to fight or use violent force.

Parable	A story or saying comparing the Kingdom of God with everyday human events.
Persecution	Harassment or ill-treatment on grounds of religious beliefs.
Pharisee	A Jewish religious teacher who taught strict obedience to the Law.
Prejudice	Holding an irrational view against someone or some people.
Prophet	A person chosen by God to speak God's message to the people.
Repentance	A sincere change of heart.
Resurrection	Rising to new life from the dead.
Sabbath	The Jewish day of rest.
Sacrifice	Giving up something for something of greater value.
Salvation	Being saved and brought into a relationship with God.
Sanhedrin	The Jewish ruling council.
Sin	Disobeying God and separating oneself from Him.
Sinai/Horeb	The mountain of God.
Son of God	The title describing Jesus' unique relationship with God.
Son of Man	The title describing Jesus' role as the one who would suffer for others.
Stewardship	Looking after the world for God.
Temptation	The desire to do something wrong.
Transfiguration	A change in a person's appearance.
Wisdom	The ability to distinguish between good and evil.
Worship	Giving God praise and honour.

Learn the following words and ideas also to help you with the longer questions.

A Rocha	A Christian charitable organisation dedicated to improving our awareness of the environment through education and sponsoring projects.
Abraham	Called by God to travel from Ur in Mesopotamia to settle in Canaan around 1800 BC. God promised Abraham that he would have many descendants. Abraham was the first to believe in one God.
Adam	Created by God using dust of the earth. God breathed life into him.
Agape	The Greek word for love which is used to refer to the generous love Jesus frequently taught about.
Angels	God's messengers who are neither human nor divine.
Apostles	'Those who are sent' – refers to Jesus' disciples' role after his death of preaching Christianity in and outside Palestine.
Baptism	The symbolic moment when sins are washed away and a person starts a new life. Jesus' baptism marked the start of his preaching ministry.
Cain and Abel	The sons of Adam and Eve. Cain grew crops and Abel looked after animals. Cain killed Abel.
Church	Refers to all Christians worldwide. Over the centuries the Church has divided itself into denominations such as the Roman Catholic, Orthodox and Protestant.
Cicely Saunders	1918–2005. A doctor who pioneered helping those with terminal illnesses. She founded St Christopher's Hospice in 1967. She believed euthanasia is wrong because it does not respect a person's value and can cause families great distress.
Creationism	The belief that Genesis gives a reliable account of the origins of the universe and that evolutionary views are wrong.
David	Succeeded King Saul around 1000 BC and died in 965 BC. As a child he defeated the Philistine strong man Goliath and later was highly regarded as a warrior.

Although he had an affair with Bathsheba, which the prophet Nathan strongly condemned, he established Israel as a strong and stable society.

Dietrich Bonhoeffer

1906–1945. A German Lutheran pastor who had to choose between an academic career in the USA and helping in his Church against the Nazi regime under Hitler. He helped found the Confessing Church which trained people in secret. He was also involved in the plot to kill Hitler. The plotters were all sent to concentration camps and executed. He was hanged in 1945.

Elijah

The first great prophet during the time of King Ahab (mid 9th century BC). He preached a message of social justice and moral integrity. At Mount Carmel he showed that God was greater than the Canaanite god Baal. He did not die but was taken up to heaven in a fiery chariot.

Euthanasia

Literally 'a good death'. When a person asks a doctor to help them to die (usually because they are very ill).

Eve

Created from Adam using one of his ribs.

Evolution

The scientific belief that all life forms have evolved from simpler forms.

Fair Trade

An international movement which makes sure that producers in poorer countries are paid a fair wage for their products.

Hypocrisy

Saying one thing but doing another, or pretending outwardly to believe something but actually believing something else.

Isaiah

Came from a wealthy Jerusalem family and was married with two children when in 742 BC God called him to deliver His word to the people of Judah. He preached for over 40 years up until the time when the Assyrians invaded Judah and laid siege to Jerusalem in 701 BC.

Jackie Pullinger

Born 1944. Felt called by God to work in the Walled City in Hong Kong. She founded a youth club to help those with drug addiction.

Jezebel

Wife of King of Ahab who encouraged the worship of the Canaanite god Baal.

Kingdom of God

God's rule on earth of justice and peace. It may also indicate a perfect state after death (heaven).

Martin Luther King	1929–1968. A black Baptist minister who led a movement to overcome the unjust laws which segregated blacks and whites in the USA. He believed in non-violent protest and arranged a bus boycott, demonstrations and a march of thousands to Washington. He was assassinated in 1968.
Martyrdom	The example set by some when they are prepared to die for their beliefs.
Mary Magdalene	One of Jesus' closest women followers, the first to arrive at Jesus' tomb and meet the resurrected Jesus.
Meg Guillebaud	Brought up in Rwanda but was ordained a priest in Britain. She returned in 1995 to help in a country torn apart by the massacre of the Tutsi people by the Hutsu tribe. She helped people from both groups by reconciling them to each other and overcoming their prejudices and fears.
Miracle on the River Kwai	A book by Ernest Gordon which describes how a British prisoner of war in Japan working on the Burma railway allowed himself to be killed by a guard to save the lives of hundreds of others. This happened when the guard thought a prisoner had stolen a spade.
Moses	Led the children of Israel out of Egypt and was given the Law (or Torah) by God at Sinai.
Mother Teresa	1910–1997. An Irish Catholic nun who moved to India to help the homeless and poorest people in Calcutta. She started schools and a special town for lepers and founded Nirmal Hriday to help the dying.
Nathan	A prophet and advisor to King David. After his criticism of David's affair with Bathsheba, Nathan became involved in a plot to establish Solomon as king in succession to David.
Oscar Romero	1917–1980. Was Catholic Archbishop of San Salvador, in Latin America. He became aware of the great gap between the very rich landowners and the poor who lived in slums. He sided with the poor and spoke for them. This made him enemies in the Church and in the government. He was shot while saying mass in 1980.
Paranormal experiences	Experiences of having visions of people who have died, or near death experiences where the soul leaves the body for a while at death and then returns shortly afterwards.

Pentecost	A Jewish festival and also the time when the apostles received the Holy Spirit. Pentecost in Christian terms is the birth of the Church.
Persecution	Being imprisoned, unfairly treated and even killed for one's beliefs.
Peter	One of Jesus' closest disciples. Although he denied knowing Jesus, he eventually became the first leader of the Church.
Pilate	The Roman governor who condemned Jesus to death by crucifixion.
Racism	An irrational hatred of people of other races. This can lead to discrimination, persecution and even killing.
Ransom	The way Jesus described his role as a sacrifice to 'pay off' the punishment for human sin and bring humans back to God.
Reconciliation	Helping people overcome their differences and be united with one another. In Christian terms it also refers to Jesus' death which brought humans back into a relationship with God.
Redemption	A state of forgiveness and being at one with God.
Saul	King in ancient Israel (1025–1000 BC). He suffered from depression and was jealous of David's success.
Sermon on the Mount	Where Jesus gave some of his most important moral and religious teaching, e.g. on loving one's enemies and the importance of forgiveness.
Solomon	Succeeded David as king in 965 BC and ruled until 928 BC. He expanded Israel's borders and brought wealth and stability to the land. He built the great Temple in Jerusalem and was renowned for his great wisdom.
Ten Commandments	The ten basic religious and moral laws given to Moses at Sinai.
The Good Samaritan	The Samaritans were despised by many Jews, but in Jesus' parable he is the only one who truly carries out God's command to love one's neighbour.
The Lost Son	In Jesus' parable, the younger son is an example of one who repents and is forgiven by God.

The serpent	Represents doubt and uncertainty in the Garden of Eden. He suggested that Eve should eat from the Tree of Knowledge.
The Sower and the Seed	In Jesus' parable the different types of ground refer to the way in which Christianity is received by different people.
The Temple	The most sacred building in ancient Israel. It was started by David, completed by Solomon, destroyed in 586 BC and built again by Herod the Great in the time of Jesus.
Transfiguration	The time when Jesus' body was transformed and the disciples saw him in his divine state and realised he was God's son.
Trevor Huddleston	1913–1998. An Anglican priest who worked in a township outside Johannesburg, South Africa. He campaigned against apartheid which segregated blacks from whites and campaigned for better housing and education for black people. He was an active supporter of the ANC (African National Congress) which, after his death, managed to abolish apartheid.
Turin Shroud	An ancient cloth with the image of a crucified man burnt on it as a negative image. Many think Jesus was buried in it and the image was caused by the power of the Resurrection.
Zacchaeus	A tax collector who, after meeting Jesus, promised not to cheat people and offered to pay back everything he had stolen, plus interest.

Summary

You should now know the following:

1. The main words to be tested in the short Part (a) questions.

2. The main words and ideas used in longer questions.

Chapter 2: Interpreting the Old Testament

The biblical texts in **Section 1** of the examination are placed in **two groups** according to **two broad themes**.

- The **first theme** is 'God, human nature and covenant'. The questions will ask you about the nature of God (e.g. His justness, omnipotence, loving kindness), human nature (e.g. selfishness, free will, wisdom, generosity) and the covenant (i.e. the promise made between God and His people and how it is to be kept). There are two questions set on this group of texts.

- The **second theme** is 'Leaders and prophets of the Old Testament'. The questions will ask you about the nature of prophecy and the main historical events in which prophets and kings had to make their decisions. You will be asked to think about their characters and ideas. There are two questions set in this group of texts.

You may decide to revise both groups to give yourself a choice of four questions or you may prefer to revise only one group of texts, in which case you will be limited to a choice of two questions.

Whatever you decide you must answer **one question** from Section 1.

Group 1: God, human nature and covenant

2.1 The Creation

Read: Genesis 1: 1–2: 25

Short questions

From the official vocabulary list, questions might be asked such as:

Q. What is stewardship?

A. Looking after the world for God

Q. What is the Sabbath?

A. Jewish day of rest

Summary of the story

In the **First Creation** story:

- In the beginning God created the heavens and the earth.

- Nothing had any shape or form.

- On the **first day** God created **light**, which He called day.

- On the **second day** God **separated the waters** and created the **sky**.

- On the **third day** God created **land**, **seas** and **plants**.

- On the **fourth day** God created the **stars**, the **sun** and **moon**.

- On the **fifth day** God created **birds** and **sea creatures**.

- On the **sixth day** God created **land animals**. He created **human beings** in His **own image**.

- God gave humans **responsibility** over all creatures.

- God commanded humans to **increase**, and **rule** the earth.

- God completed His work on the **seventh day** and **rested**. He made this a holy day.

In the **Second Creation** story:

- Before any shrub had appeared, God created **man** or Adam.

- God made **Adam** from the **dust of the earth** and **breathed** life into him.

- God planted a garden called **Eden**.

- In the middle of Eden there were **two trees**: the tree of **life** and the tree of **knowledge** of good and evil.

- God placed Adam in Eden and told him to care for it but **not to eat** from the tree of knowledge.

- God created a **helper**, **Eve**, for Adam so he should not be alone.

- God put Adam into a deep sleep and took one of his **ribs** from which he created woman, **Eve**.

Key ideas

Most scholars think that the two creation stories were written at different times and therefore make slightly different points.

The **First Creation** story teaches that there is a God-given order and design of the universe:

- God is a majestic **creator** and creates just by **commanding**.

- Humans are given control over creation because they are made in **God's image** and share in His power.

- Humans have a responsibility to **steward** and maintain the God-given order of the world.

- Everything has its proper **place** in the creation.

The **Second Creation** story concentrates on humans and their relationship with God:

- The relationship between man and God is based on **love**. God cares enough for man to provide him with a companion, woman.

- God breathes only into man, not other creatures, because it shows how much **humans share in God's nature**.

- Men and women have **a natural sexual attraction** to each other which is why they marry and have children.

Contemporary issues and evaluation

(i) Science and creation

Read pages 100–102 on science and religion when preparing this part.

Sample question

Q. Do modern theories of the origins of the universe such as the Big Bang contradict Genesis?

Points to consider:

On the one hand... some agree that because some scientists suggest that the creation of the universe happened by **chance**, there is **no need for God**.

On the other hand... others argue that **God** could have been the **cause** of the Big Bang. They suggest that the laws of physics cannot have come from nowhere, and that the initial conditions of the universe must have been set up by God.

Sample question

Q. Does evolution suggest that humans are not specially created by God?

Points to consider:

On the one hand... some argue that humans could have evolved as part of **God's plan**; evolution could still be aiming to produce conscious human life.

On the other hand... others, such as creationists, disagree because they believe there is **no firm evidence** that humans evolved from lower life forms – that there are many 'missing links' between simple life forms, apes and humans – and that God must have specially created such an intelligent animal.

Sample question

Q. Does modern science contradict the Bible?

Points to consider:

On the one hand... some **Christian creationists** argue that science is less trustworthy than the Bible, as science has not proved where we come from; that science often changes its views and sometimes contradicts itself and that Genesis explains things better and also explains **why** the universe and humans exist.

On the other hand... progressive Christians argue that science tells us **how** things might have happened, but that science is **complemented** by religion which asks **why** things happen in terms of purpose and meaning.

Sample question

Q. Does the universe have a meaning?

Points to consider:

On the one hand... some argue that as the universe is very well **designed** it has a meaning given to it by God. As Genesis suggests, the world is ordered, beautiful and things appear to **work well**.

On the other hand... many **atheists** and **humanists** argue that it is we who give the universe meaning and impose order on disorder; that we like to see patterns in nature when in fact there are none and that **suffering** suggests that if God did design the universe, then **He did it very badly**.

✏️ *Your turn*

Now try the sample questions on pages 15 and 16 yourself.

(ii) Stewardship and the environment

Read pages 102–104 on stewardship and the environment when preparing this part.

Sample question

Q. Is there a duty to steward or to rule over the environment?

Points to consider:

On the one hand... some argue that we have a duty to maintain the **natural balance** of nature, as suggested in Genesis 1 – that means thinking 'green'.

On the other hand... others argue that humans have always used the environment for their own use and that nature has a way of **balancing** herself.

Sample question

Q. Is the environment there for us to use as we wish?

Points to consider:

On the one hand... some argue that, as humans are **competitive**, then the environment is for us to use to survive and for our own purposes.

On the other hand... others argue that as humans are naturally **generous** and because we are closely related to animals then we have a duty to treat the environment with respect, not only for ourselves and animals but also for plant forms which sustain our existence.

Sample question

Q. Should we try to reduce global warming?

Points to consider:

On the one hand... some argue that Genesis teaches that as **stewards** of the world we should make every effort to reduce **global warming** through recycling, reduction of carbon gases etc.

On the other hand... others argue that the **world has undergone many climate changes** in the past and that those who say that humans have caused global warming are doing so just to make us scared and to sell products (e.g. solar panels) and make money.

Your turn

Now try the sample questions on pages 17 and 18 yourself.

2.2 The Garden of Eden and the Fall

Read: Genesis 3

Short questions

From the official vocabulary list, questions might be asked such as:

Q. What is sin?

A. Disobeying God and being separated from Him

Summary of the story

- The **serpent** tempted the woman to eat from the **Tree of Knowledge**.
    - The serpent told Eve that she would not die if she ate from the tree but she would become like God and **know good and evil**.
- **Eve** took some **fruit** from the tree and ate it.
    - She gave some to Adam.
    - When they ate it they became aware they were **naked** and they made themselves clothes.
- When they **heard God** walking in the garden they **hid**.
    - Adam said to God they had hidden because they were naked.
    - God asked him whether he had eaten from the Tree of Knowledge.

- **Adam** said that Eve had given him some fruit from it.

- Eve said the serpent had deceived her.

- God **punished** the **serpent** by making him crawl on his belly and caused **humans** to be scared of him and try to kill him.

- God punished the woman by making **childbirth** painful and making her husband **rule over her**.

- God punished the man by making **work painful**.

- God made clothes for Adam and Eve and then **expelled** them from the Garden of Eden.

- God protected the **Tree of Life** by placing cherubim and a flashing sword round it.

Key ideas

- **Eden** means 'delight' and describes a paradise where everyone and everything works in **harmony**.

- Eating from the **Tree of Knowledge** means being able to survive on one's own without being **obedient** to God.

- Only God can be self made without creating evil. Humans are unable to have this knowledge and remain good.

- The **serpent** symbolises **human desire**, **rebelliousness** and **deceitfulness**.

- Eve's act symbolises human **desire for power**.

- Adam's act symbolises human **weakness** as he gives in to Eve.

- **Nakedness** symbolises **shame** and **conscience**. Adam and Eve know what they have done is wrong.

- The **punishments** symbolise the effects of **sin**. Sin means to cut one's self off from God, which is why Adam and Eve are **expelled** from Eden.

- The physical punishments symbolise the **pain** and suffering of ordinary life; the **inequality** of men and women's relationships; the **struggle** between humans and nature to survive.

Contemporary issues and evaluation

Read pages 104–108 on human rights, law and rules when preparing this part.

Sample question

Q. Are men and women equal?

Points to consider:

On the one hand... some argue that men and women are equal because they are both **equally intelligent** and, given the same opportunities, both can achieve the **same results**.

On the other hand... others argue that because men and women are **physically different** and also have very **different emotions**, they are not equal and should be treated differently.

Sample question

Q. Are we always responsible for the consequences of our actions?

Points to consider:

On the one hand... some say that as humans have **free will** we must always take the blame for our bad actions; we cannot use our upbringing or environment as an excuse.

On the other hand... others say that human nature is **flawed** and as we are weak-willed, we cannot always be blamed for the bad things we do. They also argue that our characters are affected by our education, the society we live in, etc., so we cannot control who we are, we cannot be blamed if we have been conditioned to do bad things.

Q. Are humans naturally generous?

Points to consider:

On the one hand... some argue for a **liberal** view, that humans are naturally good but that our environment and upbringing **distorts** our naturally good nature.

On the other hand... others consider that all humans are **deeply selfish** and that because biologically we are programmed to survive, we never perform entirely generous actions. They think that the story of the Fall indicates that humans are sinful, competitive and sometimes dangerous.

Sample question

Q. Is obedience to those in authority always good?

Points to consider:

On the one hand... some feel that if we fail to carry out the commands of those in authority, then society might fall into **chaos**. Some think that leaders are there because **God appointed them**, and that therefore we have a duty to obey them, even if they are bad.

On the other hand... others argue that obedience to those in authority is only good if their **commands are good**. They argue that obedience to **bad commands** is not justified and out of **conscience** we should disobey them, even if this causes problems.

Sample question

Q. Should one always tell the truth?

Points to consider:

On the one hand... some say that telling the truth requires **courage** and is a sign of a person's strength of **character**. They say that telling the truth is always better in the **long term**, even if it causes **short-term** harm.

On the other hand... others argue that lying is sometimes justified if the **intentions** for doing so are good and it can be seen that overall **more long-term good** is achieved.

Your turn

Now try the sample questions on pages 20 and 21 yourself.

2.3 Cain and Abel

Read: Genesis 4: 1–16

Short questions

From the official vocabulary list, questions might be asked such as:

Q. What is sin?

A. Disobeying God and separating oneself from Him

Q. What is sacrifice?

A. Giving up something for something of greater value

Summary of the story

- **Eve** gave birth to **Cain** and **Abel**.
  - Abel was a **shepherd**.
  - Cain grew **crops**.
- **Abel** offered sacrifices of **animals** to God which **God was pleased with**.
- **Cain** offered sacrifices of **crops** to God which **did not please God**.
  - **Cain** was **angry**.
  - God told Cain to control his anger otherwise sin, which was '**crouching at the door**', would overcome him.
- In the field **Cain killed Abel**.
  - When God asked Cain where his brother was, Cain answered that he was not his '**brother's keeper**'.
  - God replied that Abel's blood was crying from the ground and he would therefore **punish** Cain by making it impossible for him to grow crops successfully.
  - God punished Cain further by making him **wander the earth**.
- However, God **protected** Cain from being killed by placing a '**mark**' on him.

Key ideas

- Cain and Abel offered **sacrifices** as signs of their gratitude to God.

- God **rejected** Cain's offering because Cain's **motives** were bad. Cain was often angry and selfish.

- **Sin** is described like a demon waiting to pounce. Today this might be described in **psychological** terms to mean Cain has deep-seated anger.

- **Abel's blood** crying out refers to his **innocence**. Blood is also a symbol of **life**.

- The story teaches us a lot about the **nature of God**. God knows human thoughts and motives. He **desires** genuine worship from the heart. He punishes **fairly** (Cain could have been killed for the murder of Abel). He **cares** for the innocent. He **generously** gives people second chances.

- Cain's **wandering** explains the problems encountered in ancient societies between **city dwellers** and **nomads**.

Contemporary issues and evaluation

Read pages 109–110 on aims and purpose of punishment and pages 113–114 on the abuse of power when preparing this part.

Sample question

Q. Should murderers receive the death penalty?

Points to consider:

On the one hand... some argue that as punishments must **fit the crime**, then the death penalty is reasonable and fair for horrendous crimes. Retributive justice means paying back harm with harm.

On the other hand... others argue that people must be given a **second chance**. They say that as all life is sacred, even those who commit terrible crimes should not be killed.

Your turn

Now try the sample questions on pages 23 and 24 yourself.

2.4 The near sacrifice of Isaac

Read: Genesis 22: 1–19

Short questions

From the official vocabulary list, questions might be asked such as:

Q. What is sacrifice?

A. Giving up something for something of greater value

Summary of the story

- God decided to **test Abraham**.

- Abraham was told to take his son **Isaac** to Mount Moriah and **sacrifice** him as a burnt offering.

- Early in the morning, Abraham set off with wood to make the fire for the burnt sacrifice.

- He left the servants behind and took Isaac to worship God.

- Isaac **carried the wood** and Abraham took the **knife**.

- Isaac asked why, if they had wood and fire, there was **no lamb** for the sacrifice.

- Abraham said **God would provide** the lamb.

- Abraham built the altar, **bound Isaac** and put him on top of the wood.

- As Abraham was about to kill Isaac, an **angel** told him to stop and that God now knew of Abraham's faith.

- Abraham saw a **ram caught by its horns in a bush** and he offered the ram as a sacrifice instead.

- The angel called a second time that God would bless Abraham and make his **descendants as numerous as stars** in the sky and sand on the seashore.

- God also promised that He would give Abraham **land**.

Key ideas

- There were many kinds of **sacrifices** in the ancient world. A sacrifice was a means of pleasing or thanking God using food, produce or an animal.

- An **animal sacrifice** was the greatest offering because its **blood** represented **life**.

- An **atonement sacrifice** was a special sacrifice to God in the hope that He would **forgive the sins** of a person or people.

- God's command of Abraham was a **test**: it tested his **obedience** to God; it tested whether he was prepared to make the **ultimate sacrifice** of his son as a form of animal sacrifice.

- The action of the **angel** shows that atonement sacrifices should be based on **genuine faith**.

- The **covenant** of people and land is God's **promise** and reward for faith.

- **God's voice** might be explained today as our **conscience**.

Contemporary issues and evaluation

Read page 110 on conscience, reason and morality and pages 106–107 on laws and rules when preparing this part.

Sample question

Q. Should we always obey our conscience?

Points to consider:

On the one hand... some, such as Bonhoeffer, argue that some situations are so **evil**, such as Hitler's killing of the Jews, that obedience to conscience means disobeying the law for the **greater good**.

On the other hand... others argue that conscience is **unreliable** and could just be our own **selfish desires** 'speaking' to us. They argue that if we all behaved like Bonhoeffer, law and order would **break down**.

Sample question

Q. Should we do everything which God commands?

Points to consider:

On the one hand... some say that it is always necessary to obey God because He is the **creator of the universe**.

On the other hand... others argue that God gives us **free will** to decide what is right and that we should never do something which is **bad** simply because we think God may have commanded it.

Sample question

Q. Is Abraham a good role model for us today?

Points to consider:

On the one hand... some consider that Abraham's faith and obedience has inspired many such as **William Wilberforce** who risked his reputation and helped to abolish the slave trade. He made society a better place to live in by **protecting the poor** and **weak**.

On the other hand... others think that Abraham's **blind faith** is dangerous, and the fact that he was prepared to **kill his son** shows that he is not a good role model.

Your turn

Now try the sample questions above yourself.

2.5 The Exodus and Passover

Read: Exodus 12:1–13

Short questions

From the official vocabulary list, questions might be asked such as:

Q. What does salvation mean?

A. Being saved and brought into a relationship with God

Q. What does exodus mean?

A. A way out or departure from Egypt

Q. What does sacrifice mean?

A. Giving up something for something of greater value

Q. When is the Passover lamb to be slaughtered?

A. The 14th day of the first month

Summary of the story

- God told **Moses** and **Aaron** that every Israelite family was to take a **lamb** big enough to feed each person in their household.

- The lamb had to be a one-year-old male **without defect**.

- On the **14th day of the first month** all the lambs were to be **slaughtered** at twilight.

- The **blood of the lambs** had to be painted on the **sides of the door frames** where the family was living.

- The meat had to be **roasted** and eaten with **bitter herbs**.

- They were to **eat unleavened bread**.

- All of the meat had to be **eaten before morning**.

- While they are eating, they had to be dressed as if **ready to leave** – cloak tucked in, sandals on feet, staff in hand.

- That night God would **kill all the first born** (human and animals) except those of the Israelites who had painted the blood on their door frames – He would **pass over** them.

Key ideas

- Passover marks the start of one of the key events in Israel's history, the **Exodus**. The Exodus is a sign that God sides with those who are oppressed and those who suffer injustice. During the Exodus Moses received the **Law** at Sinai. Eventually, the end of the Exodus was marked when **Joshua** brought the Israelites to the Promised Land.

- The symbol of **exodus** is used by the later prophets to describe God's **covenant relationship** with His people. Isaiah says that although God **punishes** those who stray from His commandments, He also 'leads them out' of suffering and **rewards** those who repent.

- The **first month** is Nisan (March/April in our calendar). Passover night for Jews today begins on 14 Nisan.

- God's command to **eat the lamb** at home stresses the Jewish importance of the **family**.

- Jews today place some of the roasted lamb on a plate at Passover, but it is not eaten (because there are no animal sacrifices since the destruction of the Temple in 70 CE).

- **Bitter herbs** were used to season the meat; these have come to **symbolise** the suffering of the Jews when the Jews were slaves in Egypt and all the other times they have suffered (e.g. when exiled to Babylon in 586 BCE and during the Holocaust).

- **Unleavened bread** is a reminder that there was no time to bake bread with yeast. It was also eaten at the beginning of the spring barley harvest and therefore symbolises **new beginnings**. The Jews also remove leaven as an offering to God and a sign of **sacrifice** or dedication.

- Eating the **meal in haste** is in contrast to eating during Passover today, when Jews are encouraged to lean on the table as a sign of being free. Passover reminds people that **freedom** is one of the most important aspects of human society and is not to be taken for granted.

- God's **passing over** the Israelites is a sign of God's love and **generosity** which the later prophets considered to be a characteristic of His **covenant** relationship with Israel.

Contemporary issues and evaluation

Read pages 114–117 on social justice when preparing this part.

Sample question

Q. Should God take sides?

Points to consider:

On the one hand... some argue that God should not take sides because this suggests that He favours some people more than others and He is **supposed to love all people equally**. They argue that if God is a god of justice then to be biased towards some people more than others shows that He cannot really be omnipotent (all powerful) because He is acting emotionally, like a human being.

On the other hand... others say that if justice means righting wrongs, then it means treating those who have suffered unfairly first. They say that this is what it means for God to take sides – that He is a **just and generous** God who is prepared to be involved in **human history**.

Sample question

Q. Can the Passover, which happened 3000 years ago, teach us anything today?

Points to consider:

On the one hand... some argue that the Passover is a powerful story about leadership, bravery, risk-taking and trust and therefore can continue to **inspire** Jews and non-Jews alike. They argue that Jesus used the Passover symbols to teach about the meaning of his sacrificial death. Some also point out that **Martin Luther King** used the Exodus/Passover idea to inspire the people to march to Washington to **protest against racial injustice**.

On the other hand... others say that life 3000 years ago was very different and the Passover is **unrealistic** in terms of how we can achieve justice today. They say, for example, that painting blood on doorposts and eating unleavened bread sounds more like **magic** than genuine religious behaviour. They also say that it seems **unfair** that innocent Egyptian children and animals should have died simply because they did not carry out these strange commands.

Your turn

Now try the sample questions above yourself.

2.6 The Ten Commandments

Read: Exodus 19: 1–8; Exodus 20: 1–17

Short questions

From the official vocabulary list, questions might be asked such as:

Q. What is meant by covenant?

A. An agreement between God and His people

Q. What is meant by Sabbath?

A. The Jewish day of rest

Q. What is Sinai?

A. The mountain of God

Q. What is sin?

A. Disobeying God and separating oneself from Him

Summary of the story

- In the Sinai desert God called **Moses** up the **mountain**.

- Moses was told to tell the Israelites how God had rescued them from Egypt on **'eagles' wings'**.

- They were to keep God's covenant and become a **holy nation**.

- Moses went down the mountain and gave the Israelites God's words.

- When Moses went up the mountain again, God gave Moses the **Ten Commandments**:

  1. You shall have **no other gods**.
  2. You shall **not make any idols**.
  3. You shall **not misuse God's name**.
  4. You shall keep the **Sabbath day holy** by working six days and resting on the seventh.
  5. You shall **honour your father and mother**.
  6. You shall **not murder**.
  7. You shall **not commit adultery**.
  8. You shall **not steal**.
  9. You shall **not give false witness**.
  10. You shall **not envy or covet** (your neighbour's wife, his servants, his possessions).

Key ideas

- The Ten Commandments form the heart of God's **covenant** with Israel.

- A **holy nation** means a nation which is specially chosen by God to be an example to the world.

- God has rescued Israel from Egypt as a sign of His **love**.

- The commands are the ten most important of the **613 commandments** of the Law which God gave to Moses.

- The commandments are on **two tablets**: 1–4 are **religious duties**; 5–10 are **social and moral duties**.

- **Commandment 1**: Judaism is a **monotheism** (worship of one God) which also means there is only **one form of morality** (knowing what is good and bad).

- **Commandment 2**: as God is **not a thing** then **no earthly thing** or human made thing can be a source of power or **authority**.

- **Commandment 3**: making a **promise** (using God's name) means it **cannot be broken.** Misusing God's name is also called blasphemy (making oneself equal or greater than God).

- **Commandment 4**: remembers God's **creation** and stops the **exploitation** of workers by giving them a day of rest.

- **Commandment 5**: recognises parents as a source of **wisdom** and **authority**.

- **Commandment 6**: life is **sacred** because it is God-given. **Deliberate killing**, unless authorised by God (as in war or capital punishment), is **morally wrong**.

- **Commandment 7**: **wives** were seen as the **property of husbands**, so adultery is a form of theft.

- **Commandment 8**: stealing destroys people's **livelihood** and **trust** of one another. The heart of the covenant is trust.

- **Commandment 9**: as many crimes were punished using the **death penalty,** making a false statement about someone was serious.

- **Commandment 10**: in small communities **respect for property** is essential; envy breaks down **trust** and the stability of society.

Contemporary issues and evaluation

Read pages 104–110 on human rights, law and rules when preparing this part.

Q. Should the aim of punishment be to deter others?

Points to consider:

On the one hand... some argue that unless punishments are **severe** then no one will take them **seriously**.

On the other hand... others say that the aim of punishment is to **reform** those who have done wrong so that they become **good members** of society again.

Sample question

Q. Should the aim of punishment be to make wrongdoers suffer?

Points to consider:

On the one hand... some agree that punishment should cause the criminal to suffer so that the people who have suffered from a crime can **feel justice** has been carried out.

On the other hand... others argue that many (including Jesus and Gandhi) felt that retribution makes society **morally weak** and that true justice comes from **compassion**.

Sample question

Q. Should murderers always receive the death penalty?

Points to consider:

On the one hand... some argue that as punishments must **fit the crime** then the death penalty is reasonable and fair. They argue that retributive justice ('an eye for an eye') is important because it is society's means of showing what is not acceptable.

On the other hand... others argue that people must be given a **second chance**. They argue that the death penalty does not allow for repentance, degrades society and does not actually reduce the incidence of crimes such as murder.

Q. Is the most important right the right to life?

Points to consider:

On the one hand... some argue that the right to life is the **basis** for many other rights such as respect for property, the right to free speech etc. because the right to life means having a good **quality** of life.

On the other hand... others think that this is too vague and that rights have to be based on other things such as **freedom**, **happiness** and **protection**. An example of this is in the **United Nations Declaration of Human Rights**.

 Your turn

Now try the sample questions on pages 32 and 33 yourself.

Group 2: Leaders and prophets of the Old Testament

2.7 Moses

Read: Exodus 3:1–17

Short questions

From the official vocabulary list, questions might be asked such as:

Q. What does salvation mean?

A. Being saved and brought into relationship with God

Q. What does exodus mean?

A. A way out or departure from Egypt

Q. What is Horeb?

A. The mountain of God

Summary of the story

- Moses was tending **Jethro's** (his father-in-law's) **sheep**.

- He led them to **Horeb**.

- God's angel appeared in the **flames of a bush.**

- The bush was **not destroyed** by the flames.

- God called to Moses from the bush '**Moses! Moses!**'.

- Moses said '**Here I am**'.

- God told Moses to take **off his sandals** because he was on **holy ground**.

- God said He was the **God of Abraham, Isaac and Jacob**.

- Moses **hid his face**; he was afraid to look at God.

- God said He had seen the suffering of the Israelites in Egypt and had **come to rescue them**.

- He promised to lead them to a land '**flowing with milk and honey**'.

- Moses was to **go to Pharaoh** and bring the Israelites out of Egypt.

- Moses asked why he should do this.

- God answered that **He would be with Moses** and when he had rescued the people they would worship him at Horeb.

- Moses asked what he should do if the people asked for **God's name**.

- God told Moses to tell the Israelites that '**I am who I am**' had sent him.

- God told Moses to tell the people about **His promise** to take them to a new land.

Key ideas

- This is one of the most important moments in Exodus because **Moses learns of his mission** as **prophet** and **leader**; also, for the first time **God reveals His name**.

- Taking one's **shoes off** is a sign of respect for God; Moses recognises that this is a **holy place**.

- At first Moses learns that this God is the **god of his ancestors** (Abraham, Isaac and Jacob). Then he learns that God **is far greater** than this and that he just 'is' – God is **unique** and there is **nothing else like Him**.

- 'I am' can also be translated as '**I will be what I will be**' and implies that God is **eternal** and can **never fully be understood by humans** and that He has future plans for humans which are as yet a **mystery**.

- The ancient Israelites believed that **knowing the name** of a god was a means of being able to call on him to **act**.

- The 'land flowing with milk and honey' is **Canaan**. God's covenant promise with the Israelites will be to give them a land like **Eden**. This represents God's generous nature and love.

- Moses is shown being **hesitant and unsure**; he needs reassurance from God.

Contemporary issues and evaluation

Read page 113 on leadership and authority when preparing this part.

Sample question

Q. Can we ever know God?

Points to consider:

On the one hand... some argue that we can never know God because He is by definition **greater than the human mind can conceive**. They argue that we might be able to know **about God** from miracles or answers to prayer but this never tells us much about who He really is.

On the other hand... others say that God **reveals** aspects of Himself to His prophets such as Moses or Isaiah. Christians believe that in Jesus Christ humans are able to **know about God's love** in a new way. They say that knowing about God means having a relationship with him, which can only be achieved because **God chooses** to be involved with humans.

Sample question

Q. Is the story of Moses at the burning bush the most important moment in the Old Testament?

Points to consider:

On the one hand... some argue that it is because it is the first time **God reveals His true nature** and calls Moses to start the Exodus. Without these two things the Israelites would not have become a **great nation**, the Law would not have been given to Moses and this key event would not have inspired the later prophets.

On the other hand... others say that it is not because the giving of the **Law at Sinai** was the first moment when the Israelites could think of themselves as a civilized nation with a **code to live by**.

Your turn

Now try the sample questions on page 35 yourself.

2.8 David and Bathsheba

Read: 2 Samuel 11: 1–17

Short questions

From the official vocabulary list, questions might be asked such as:

Q. What is sin?

A. Disobeying God and being separated from Him

Q. What is temptation?

A. The desire to do something wrong

Summary of the story

- One evening in spring **David** could see a **beautiful woman bathing** on her roof.

- He found out that she was **Bathsheba**, wife of **Uriah the Hittite**.

- David had sex with her and then, later, found she was **pregnant**.

- David told **Joab** to send **Uriah** home to report on the war to him.

- He hoped he would **sleep** with Bathsheba but Uriah slept at the **door of the palace**.

- Uriah said he could not go home whilst his **men were fighting**.

- The next evening David got Uriah **drunk**, but Uriah **slept with the servants**.

- David sent a letter to Joab telling him to place Uriah in the **front line of the battle** and then to withdraw his troops so Uriah would be killed.

- Joab did as he was told and **Uriah was killed**.

- David was now **free to marry** Bathsheba.

Key ideas

- The proper role of the king was to **protect**, to be a **'shepherd of the people'**.

- David's affair with Bathsheba shows his **misuse of power**.

- David was ruled by **lust** and emotion, **not reason**, when he sent Uriah to his death.

- **Uriah's** character **contrasts** to **David's**.

- Uriah is loyal, trustworthy and loving.

- David is lustful, devious and dishonest.

Contemporary issues and evaluation

Read page 113 on leadership and authority, page 110 on conscience, reason and morality and pages 113–114 on the abuse of power when preparing this part.

Sample question

Q. Should one always obey the law even if the law is bad?

Points to consider:

On the one hand… some argue that we cannot always see the bigger picture and to disobey the law whenever we feel like it might lead to **anarchy**. Uriah obeyed David for this reason.

On the other hand… others argue that we should protest against unfair laws. **Martin Luther King** led a campaign of **civil disobedience** in America because of the laws which discriminated against black people and in the end he won.

Sample question

Q. Is a good leader one who puts people first?

Points to consider:

On the one hand… some argue that a leader should use his **talents** to **serve** others first, just as David should have been a shepherd to the people.

On the other hand… others think that a leader is there to put the law, justice, business or **the cause first**. Business people, for example, have to make their businesses a **success** otherwise everyone loses.

Your turn

Now try the sample questions on pages 37 and 38 yourself.

2.9 Nathan

Read: 2 Samuel 12: 1–14

Short questions

From the official vocabulary list, questions might be asked such as:

Q. What is a prophet?

A. A person chosen by God to speak God's message to the people

Q. What is a parable?

A. A story or saying comparing the Kingdom of God with everyday human events

Summary of the story

- God sent **Nathan** to **David** to tell him a parable.
    - In the parable there were two men, **one rich** and **one poor**.
    - The rich man had a **lot of sheep** but the poor man had only **one little ewe lamb**.
    - The ewe lamb was loved and part of the family, '**it was like a daughter to him**'.
    - One day the rich man had to entertain a traveller but he did not want to use his own sheep so **he took the poor man's lamb** and prepared it for dinner.
- When David heard the parable he was very angry and said the **rich man should die**.

- Nathan said, '**You are that man!**'

- Nathan told David that as king he should not have killed Uriah and slept with Bathsheba.

- Nathan told David that God would now punish him: he would see his wives taken away by one of his friends.

- David confessed that he had **sinned**.

- Nathan said that **God** would now **forgive** him; he would not die, but his **son would die instead**.

Key ideas

- Nathan was not only a **prophet** but acted as the **king's trusted advisor** and his **conscience**.

- Nathan **protected** David right up until David's death. He plotted with Bathsheba to make Solomon king after David (1 Kings 1).

- Nathan's parable was not intended to be a direct parallel to David's situation but an **example of a gross injustice**.

- Nathan **cleverly** used the poor man's action in the parable to show how **insensitive and crude the rich man is** by comparison.

- Nathan therefore got the reaction he wanted from David by touching on his conscience.

- David did not blame Nathan for his **bold criticism** but **admired** Nathan's skill and honesty.

- Nathan pointed out that David's reaction to a lesser crime had implications for him – if the rich man deserves the **death penalty** for stealing, what should happen to David? It is only because David **repented** that he received a **lesser punishment** (not the death penalty but his wives being taken away and the death of his son with Bathsheba).

- Nathan says that God is **merciful**. **God does not desire the death of a sinner** but rather that he or she should change their way of life and live.

Contemporary issues and evaluation

Read page 113 on leadership and authority, page 108 on rights and punishment and page 108 on aims and purpose of punishment when preparing this part.

Q. Should leaders and figures in authority be punished more than ordinary people if they misuse their power?

Points to consider:

On the one hand... some think that they should be punished more because more authority means **greater responsibility**. If this responsibility is abused then the punishment should be greater.

On the other hand... others argue that the **law** and **punishments** apply to all people **equally**. Although Harold Shipman killed many patients he was not condemned to death but imprisoned as the law demands.

Q. Was David punished enough for his crimes?

Points to consider:

On the one hand... some argue that David was **responsible for Uriah's murder** and went out of his way to **commit adultery**, and that both actions should have carried the **death penalty**. Even David thought that the rich man in Nathan's parable should have been executed. They argue that as king he is not above the law.

On the other hand... others say that kings, like David, and other people with **social responsibilities** have much **greater duties** so we cannot judge them in quite the same way as we do ordinary people. They argue that David was punished enough.

Q. Is Nathan no more than David's conscience?

On the one hand... some argue that the character of Nathan is less important than the parable he tells. The moral judgements are all made by David, so Nathan is really another way of referring to David's conscience.

On the other hand... others say that later on, when David is old and weak, Nathan plays a vital role in making Solomon (David's son) king. Nathan is not just a symbol of the king's conscience. Nathan is a clever man who knows how to behave according to the situation.

Your turn

Now try the sample questions on page 40 yourself.

Now try the sample questions on page 40 yourself.

2.10 Solomon

Read: 1 Kings 3

Short questions

From the official vocabulary list, questions might be asked such as:

Q. What is the Ark of the Covenant?

A. A sacred box containing the two tablets of the Law (Ten Commandments)

Q. What is wisdom?

A. The ability to distinguish between good and evil

Q. What is justice?

A. Treating others fairly

Summary of the story

- **Solomon** kept to the **laws of God** except that he continued to make **sacrifices at the shrines**.

- One day, at the shrine of **Gibeon**, God appeared to Solomon in a **dream**.

- God asked Solomon to request whatever he would most like.

- Solomon said that he would like a '**discerning heart**' to be able to see what was right and what was wrong.

- God was pleased and said He would grant his request so Solomon would be able to rule **justly**.

- Furthermore, because he had not asked for them, He would give him great **riches and a long life**.

- Solomon returned to **Jerusalem** and made an offering at the **Ark of the Covenant**.

- One day **two prostitutes** came to Solomon, both claiming that a baby was their own:

  - One claimed that the other had accidentally lain on her own baby and suffocated it, stolen her baby and put the dead baby in its place.

  - Solomon told them to bring a sword and then ordered **the baby to be chopped in two**.

- The **real mother** shouted out for him to stop and let the other woman keep the baby.

- The false mother told the king to carry on so that neither of them could have the baby.

- Solomon gave the baby to the true mother.

- Everyone was amazed by Solomon's **wisdom** and **justice**.

Key ideas

- **Solomon** was **King David's son** and famous for his great **wealth,** his **wisdom** and building the **Temple**.

- His sacrifice at Gibeon and later in Jerusalem showed that Solomon was a **religious man**.

- **Dreams** in the ancient world were thought to be the means by which **God spoke** to humans.

- God **tested** Solomon by offering him whatever he would like.

- Solomon asked for the ability to know the **difference** between good and bad.

- **Riches** and long life are signs of God's **blessing**.

- Solomon's judgement showed his ability and **skill** to **understand** human nature; the true mother would never kill her own child.

- **Prostitutes** were low on the social scale, but Solomon **judged them fairly**.

- Solomon's story shows that **wisdom** is: **skill**, **understanding**, being open to **God's will**, putting **others first** and being **fair**.

Contemporary issues and evaluation

Read pages 113 on leadership and authority when preparing this part.

Sample question

Q. Is wisdom more than just being good?

Points to consider:

On the one hand… some think that wisdom is the ability to be **just and fair**, to know which **moral principles** to use in a situation.

On the other hand… others think that having wisdom is **being skilful**. A wise choice is one that **works**, even if it is based on cunning or a lie.

Sample question

Q. Is a good leader one who puts other people first?

Points to consider:

On the one hand... some argue that this is true because a good leader should use his or her **talents** to **serve** others. Solomon treated the needs of the two prostitutes wisely.

On the other hand... others think that a good leader should put the law, justice, business or the **cause first**. Business people, for example, have to make their business a **success** otherwise everyone loses.

Sample question

Q. Was Solomon wise or just lucky?

Points to consider:

On the one hand... some argue that it was luck that it was the real mother who asked him to stop. Solomon **could not have known** much about their characters or circumstances, so he was just **guessing**.

On the other hand... others argue that Solomon may not have known much about these women but wisdom is acquired by knowing **about human nature**. Solomon had experience of making **judgements** of this kind and knew what was likely to work in this case.

Your turn

Now try the sample questions on pages 42 and 43 yourself.

2.11 Elijah: Elijah and the prophets of Baal

Read: 1 Kings 18:19–46

Short questions

From the official vocabulary list, questions might be asked such as:

Q. What is a prophet?

A. A person chosen by God to speak God's message to the people

Q. Who is Baal?

A. A Canaanite god

Q. What is a sacrifice?

A. Giving up something for something of greater value

Summary of the story

- King **Ahab** sent the prophet **Obadiah** to **find water** during a terrible drought and famine.

- Obadiah met Elijah. **Elijah** told him to report to **Ahab** that he had met him.

- **Obadiah** was **scared** that Ahab would kill him if Elijah did not then present himself to the king.

- Elijah assured him that he would meet the king.

- When **Ahab** met Elijah, Ahab said, 'Is that you, you **troubler of Israel?**'.

- Elijah replied that the real troubler was Ahab.

- Elijah challenged 450 **prophets of Baal** and 400 **prophets of Asherah** to a contest at **Mount Carmel**.

- Elijah told the people that they had to **choose** between the worship of **God** or the worship of **Baal**.

- Two bulls were cut in pieces and placed on two piles of wood but not set alight.

- Whichever **god set the pile alight** would be the **true god**.

- The prophets of Baal called on their god, but nothing happened.

- Elijah teased them and told them to shout louder to **wake Baal up**, but nothing happened.

- Elijah built an altar of **12 stones** (one for each of the 12 tribes of Israel) and then poured **four jars of water** on the wood.

- They poured water three times.

- Elijah prayed to God; God sent **fire to consume the sacrifice**.

- The people shouted, 'The Lord – he is God!'.

- Elijah commanded that the prophets of **Baal should be killed**.

- **Elijah** went to **pray** at the top of **Mount Carmel**.

- It began to **rain** heavily.

Key ideas

- The drought had **lasted over thee years**, so many had started to worship the **Canaanite** god **Baal** who was the **god of rain**.

- **Elijah** was Israel's greatest **prophet** and believed that **only God** should be worshipped.

- **Waking up Baal** was part of usual Canaanite worship but Elijah used it to **tease** the prophets.

- The **12 stones** Elijah used symbolised the **whole nation** (10 tribes in the south and two in the north).

- Elijah's prayer was **simple** compared to those of the other prophets.

- The people's cry, that God is one, is the most important **Jewish prayer**.

- Elijah killed the prophets of Baal to **stop rumours** that Baal had lit his sacrifice and as a sign of God's **judgement** of **false worship**.

Contemporary issues and evaluation

Read pages 114–117 on social justice and pages 113–114 on leadership and authority when preparing this part.

Sample question

Q. Should violence be used to defend one's beliefs?

Points to consider:

On the one hand... some think that in some extreme cases it is right to defend one's beliefs against those who would be prepared to **harm** or even kill you. Use of force is also a **symbol** of the power of belief.

On the other hand... others think that the use violence never really persuades people. **Oscar Romero** believed that change comes through people acting together. Defending one's beliefs can even mean having to die for them, as he did.

Sample question

Q. Are celebrities today's false gods?

Points to consider:

On the one hand... some think that this is true because **no celebrity can ever live up to people's hopes and expectations.** They do not bring people real happiness.

On the other hand... others think that we like to see successful people. It **gives us hope** and they show us what humans can achieve. They are only false when they **misuse their success.**

Sample question

Q. Was Elijah a successful prophet?

Points to consider:

On the one hand... some argue that Elijah was a prophet of great **moral and social standing.** When other prophets worshipped other gods Elijah remained true to God. Elijah succeeded in showing that the polytheism of the Canaanites was ineffective.

On the other hand... others argue that Elijah's treatment of the prophets of Baal was not good. He mocked and **teased** them and then commanded **mass murder.** As a prophet of God he should have shown compassion and mercy.

Your turn

Now try the sample questions on pages 45 and 46 yourself.

2.12 Elijah: Elijah and the still small voice

Read: 1 Kings 19: 1–18

Short questions

From the official vocabulary list, questions might be asked such as:

Q. What is a prophet?

A. A person chosen by God to speak God's message to the people

Q. What is Horeb?

A. The mountain of God

Q. What is meant by covenant?

A. An agreement between God and His people

Q. Who is Baal?

A. A Canaanite god

Summary of the story

- When **Jezebel** heard how **Elijah** had **killed** the **prophets of Baal** she threatened to kill him.

- Elijah fled to the wilderness. He had had enough and prayed to God to let him die.

  - An angel woke him up and he **found a cake and a jar of water**.

  - The angel woke him again and told him to eat again for the journey.

- Elijah came to **Horeb** and **stayed in a cave**.

- God visited Elijah and asked him what he was doing.

- Elijah answered that he was the only true prophet left and now the Israelites were trying to kill him.

- God told him to stand on the mountain because He was going to '**pass by**'.

- Then a powerful **wind** blew which broke rocks – but God was not in the wind.

- Then there was an **earthquake** – but God was not in the earthquake.

- Then there was **fire** – but God was not in the fire.

- Then there was a **gentle whisper** (a still 'small voice') and it asked Elijah what he was doing.

- Elijah replied that he had tried very hard to make the people keep to the **covenant**.

- God told him to return and **anoint two kings**.

- He also told him to anoint **Elisha**.

- God told Elijah that He had protected 7000 people from worshipping Baal.

Key ideas

- **Jezebel** was the **wife** of King **Ahab**. She **encouraged** the worship of **Baal**, the chief god of the Canaanites.

- Elijah was **depressed** because God had not stopped Jezebel killing God's prophets.

- **Horeb** is a special mountain where God had **revealed** Himself in the past.

- In contrast to what was believed about Baal, God is **not found in nature** (wind, fire, earthquake).

- God is found in one's **heart**, in one's **thoughts** and in **stillness**.

- **Elisha** continued Elijah's work after **Elijah died** and was taken to heaven.

Contemporary issues and evaluation

Read pages 101–102 on God and science and pages 113–114 on leadership and authority when preparing this part.

Sample question

Q. Does God only speak to us when we are lonely?

Points to consider:

On the one hand... some argue that it is when we are lonely or sad that we are most **receptive** to God's presence. If **God is love** then we have to be aware of this in quiet or in **prayer**.

On the other hand... others argue that God can be experienced when we are lonely but equally he can be experienced **intellectually** when we think about the cause of the universe or the beauty and **design of nature**.

Sample question

Q. How can we know when God is acting in the world?

Points to consider:

On the one hand... some argue that we can know when God acts because, as God is **good**, then an event which God **causes** will always produce good.

On the other hand... others argue that it is very hard to know when God is acting in the world. An earthquake might **equally** be God's punishment or just an **unfortunate event** in nature.

Sample question

Q. How can we tell whether God is just a figment of our imagination?

Points to consider:

On the one hand... some argue that although God cannot be proved we see how God has **inspired** millions to work for **justice**, to **protect** the weak and to **produce** great art and music.

On the other hand... others argue that God is just our imagination or our inner **conscience** speaking to us and that God is an idea which keeps people from doing wrong.

 ### Your turn

Now try the sample questions on pages 48 and 49 yourself.

2.13 Isaiah

Read: Isaiah 1:10–20 and Isaiah 5:1–7

Short questions

From the official vocabulary list, questions might be asked such as:

Q. What is justice?

A. Treating others fairly

Q. What is a parable?

A. A story or saying comparing the Kingdom of God with everyday human events

Q. What is a sacrifice?

A. Giving up something for something else of greater value

Q. What is a prophet?

A. A person chosen by God to speak God's message to the people

Summary of the story

Isaiah's message to Judah:

- God said to Isaiah that:
    - the rulers of **Sodom and Gomorrah** had **failed to listen to His law**
    - though they offered sacrifices, they were meaningless and gave Him no pleasure
    - **'Stop bringing me meaningless sacrifices!'**
    - he **hated all their festivals**
    - when they tried to pray to Him, He would not listen because their **hands were 'full of blood'**
    - they needed to make themselves spiritually clean by **seeking justice** (helping the **oppressed, defending the fatherless** and **protecting widows**)
    - there was hope: **'Though your sins are like scarlet, they shall be as white as snow'**
    - if the leaders learnt to be obedient they would be rewarded, but if they did not they would be destroyed.

Song of the Vineyard:

- Isaiah introduced the song of the vineyard as a song for his lover about his vineyard:
    - His lover built a vineyard on a **fertile hillside**.
    - He **cleared all the stones** and planted it with the best vines.
    - He built a **watchtower**.
    - He built a **winepress**.
    - But the vines did **not produce good fruit**.
- He then explained the parable:
    - The people of Jerusalem and Judah were like the vineyard.
    - **God had prepared everything** for them but **they had only given Him bad results** in return.
    - Now God would take away the hedge of the vineyard and **break down the wall**.

- The **vineyard would become a wasteland** and only weeds and **thorns** would grow there.

- God would command that it **never rains there**.

- God looked for **justice** but **found bloodshed**.

- He looked for **righteousness** but 'heard **cries of distress**'.

Key ideas

- Isaiah received his visions at a time of political uncertainty when Judah (the southern kingdom) fell increasingly under Assyria's control.

- God said to Isaiah that the people were not obeying Him as dutiful children should do and they were showing him no respect.

- Although they gave **God lip service** by carrying out their religious duties, all these were meaningless because their **hearts were far from God**.

- The leaders of Israel were using religion to have a good time, and to enjoy the festivals but had failed to uphold the most basic aspect of the Law which is justice.

- The reference to the **rulers of Sodom** and the **people of Gomorrah** reinforces how bad matters were.

- Both cities were well known for their corrupt morality which included sexual exploitation, rape and murder.

- Despite the degree of Israel's sins, Isaiah's message is actually one of **hope**.

- The contrast is made between the present and the future which God offered them – when their sins would be completely removed.

- All these are ideas are re-expressed in the **parable** or **allegory** of the vineyard.

- The contrast is between God's love for Israel and her complete rejection of that love.

  - The **land** is the **land of Israel** which God promised to Abraham as part of the covenant.

  - The **vineyard** represents the **people** of Israel and Judah **whom God loves**.

  - The **bad fruit** represents the **failure of the people** to carry out God's law.

  - The **destruction** of the vineyard represents God's **judgement**.

Contemporary issues and evaluation

Read pages 114–117 on social justice, page 113 on leadership and authority and pages 113–114 on the abuse of power when preparing this part.

Sample question

Q. Have we any need for prophets today?

Points to consider:

On the one hand... some argue that we need people who are outspoken and prepared to be unpopular. A prophet is not just someone who predicts the future but someone who touches people's conscience and tells society what it is doing wrong. A prophet can speak with conviction because he or she (like Mother Teresa) feels inspired and supported by God.

On the other hand... others think that prophets are troublemakers and people should decide for themselves what is right and wrong. Isaiah said that what matters is justice, but we do not need a prophet to tell us that.

Sample question

Q. Are there some sins which are so evil they cannot be forgiven?

Points to consider:

On the one hand... some argue that there are people who have done such evil things (such as Ian Huntley who murdered Jessica Chapman and Holly Wells) that even if they showed remorse, it would be impossible to forgive them because of all the harm they have done. It would also mean that their victims would feel robbed of justice.

On the other hand... others think that all humans are capable of change and there are always reasons why people do bad things, such as poor upbringing, poverty or too much money.

Your turn

Now try the sample questions on pages 52 and 53 yourself.

Summary

You should now know the main points and ideas behind the following:

Group 1 texts:
1. The First Creation story
2. The Second Creation story
3. The Garden of Eden and the Fall
4. The story of Cain and Abel
5. Abraham's near sacrifice of Isaac
6. The Passover and Exodus from Egypt
7. The giving of the Ten Commandments at Sinai

Group 2 texts:
8. Moses' encounter with God at the burning bush
9. King David's affair with Bathsheba
10. Nathan's parable criticising David
11. Solomon's wisdom
12. The story of Elijah and the prophets of Baal
13. Elijah's experience of God as the small voice
14. Isaiah's message to Judah and the Song of the Vineyard

You should also know the main contemporary issues relating to each of these stories.

Test yourself

Before moving on to the next chapter, make sure you can answer the following questions. Sample answers are given on pages 193–195.

Group 1 texts

1. The Second Creation story

(a) Name two ways in which God punished Adam and Eve. (2)

(b) Describe the main features of the Garden of Eden. (6)

(c) Explain what the creation story teaches about human stewardship of the world. (6)

(d) 'We are not always responsible for the consequences of our actions.' Do you agree? Give reasons to support your answer. (7)

2. The Ten Commandments

(a) What is Sinai? (2)

(b) Describe any five of the Ten Commandments. (6)

(c) Explain what this story teaches about the relationship between God and humans. (6)

(d) 'The aim of any punishment is to make the wrongdoer suffer.' Do you agree? Give reasons to support your answer. (7)

Group 2 texts

3. David and Bathsheba

(a) What is temptation? (2)

(b) Describe how David came to marry to Bathsheba. (6)

(c) Explain what this story teaches about David as a ruler. (6)

(d) 'Leaders should be punished more than ordinary people if they misuse their authority.' Do you agree? Give reasons to support your answer. (7)

4. Isaiah's message

(a) What is a prophet? (2)

(b) Outline Isaiah's message of judgement against the leaders and people of Judah. (6)

(c) Explain why God considers Judah to be badly sinful and corrupt. (6)

(d) 'Isaiah's message was too harsh.' Do you agree? Give reasons to support your answer. (7)

Chapter 3: Interpreting the New Testament

The biblical texts in **Section 2** of the examination are placed in **two groups** according to **two broad themes**.

- The **first theme** is 'Jesus' teaching' and questions will ask you about his teaching about the Kingdom of God (e.g. God's rule on earth requiring repentance and forgiveness), which Jesus illustrated through the use of parables (stories and analogies) and various kinds of miracles (healing and nature miracles). You should know and understand Jesus' teaching on prejudice, attitude to wealth, treatment of the marginalised and the nature of sin. There are two questions set in this group of texts.

- The **second theme** is 'Jesus' life, death and resurrection' and questions will ask you about the main events of Jesus' life from his birth, baptism and choice of disciples to his final week before being crucified and then resurrected. You should know and understand the historical and religious background to these events. There are two questions set in this group of texts.

You may decide to revise both groups to give yourself a choice of four questions or you may prefer to revise only one group of texts, in which case you will be limited to a choice of two questions.

Whatever you decide you must answer **one question** from Section 2.

Group 1: Jesus' teaching

3.1 Zacchaeus

Read: Luke: 19: 1–10

Short questions

From the official vocabulary list, questions might be asked such as:

Q. What is meant by salvation?

A. Being saved and brought into a relationship with God

Q. What is meant by Son of Man?

A. Jesus' role as the one who would suffer for others

Q. What is meant by sacrifice?

A. Giving up something for something of greater value

Summary of the story

- Jesus was passing through **Jericho**.

- **Zacchaeus** was the **chief tax collector** and very wealthy.

- He **climbed** a sycamore **tree** to see Jesus better because he was **short**.

- When **Jesus** came to the tree he told him to **come down**.

- Jesus wanted to **stay at his house** straight away.

- The **crowd** were **annoyed** that Jesus should want to stay with a '**sinner**'.

- Zacchaeus immediately said he would give **half his possessions to the poor**.

- He said he would also **pay** all those **he had cheated four times** the amount he had stolen.

- Jesus said that Zacchaeus had received **salvation**.

- Jesus said, 'The **Son of Man** came to seek and save what was lost'.

Key ideas

- **Tax collectors** in Jesus' time were mistrusted because they worked for the Romans and often overtaxed people so they could become rich.

- **Sinners** refers to all those **excluded** from the **Jewish Law** and therefore shunned by religious people.

- **Jericho** was a **major tax point** for people entering Palestine from the east.

- Zacchaeus as chief tax collector was very rich because he had a share **in all the taxes** coming into Jericho.

- Zacchaeus' **conscience** led him to make a big effort to see Jesus and listen to his teaching.

- Zacchaeus **repented** because he knew what he had done was wrong, **not because he wanted social recognition**.

- The fact that Jesus stayed with a sinner would have **shocked** the religious people of Jericho because it would have made Jesus **religiously unclean**.

- Jesus calls himself the **Son of Man** because his role is to **represent all people to God** and prepare them for the Kingdom of God.

Contemporary issues and evaluation

Read pages 114–117 on social justice and pages 118–120 on prejudice and discrimination when preparing this part.

Sample question

Q. Do we have a duty to help outcasts today?

Points to consider:

On the one hand... some argue that often people are lonely, depressed or lose their jobs and therefore turn to drink, drugs or prostitution which can result in prison. Organisations such as the **Salvation Army** help them because the same things could happen to anyone and because all humans are equally important and equally valued.

On the other hand... others think that often people **create their own problems** through greed or weakness. They think that we **do not have a duty** to help them and should help those who are genuinely ill, old or disabled.

Sample question

Q. Did Jesus set a bad example by staying with Zacchaeus?

Points to consider:

On the one hand... some think that Jesus did set a bad example because it is wrong to mix with people who **have low moral standards** and might even be dangerous.

On the other hand... others think that Jesus judged that Zacchaeus wanted help and **he took a risk**. Helping those rejected by society can be dangerous. **Jackie Pullinger's** work in Hong Kong with drug users required a lot of courage and conviction and is a good example of **moral behaviour**.

Your turn

Now try the sample questions above yourself.

3.2 The paralysed man

Read: Mark 2: 1–12

Short questions

From the official vocabulary list, questions might be asked such as:

Q. What is a miracle?

A. An act of God which breaks the laws of physics

Q. What is sin?

A. Disobeying God and separating oneself from Him

Q. What is faith?

A. Having an active trust in someone or in God

Q. What does Son of Man mean?

A. Jesus' role as the one who would suffer for others

Q. What is blasphemy?

A. Speaking against God or making oneself equal to God

Summary of the story

- **Jesus** was at **Capernaum**.

- There were so many people there that four men who carried a **paralysed man** could not get near Jesus.

- They therefore climbed onto the **roof** of the house, dug a hole in it and **lowered the man down**.

- When Jesus saw their **faith**, he said to the paralysed man that his **sins were forgiven**.

- The **lawyers** present **criticised** Jesus and said his words were **blasphemy** – **only God can forgive sins**.

- Jesus said to them that forgiving sins and healing amounted to the same thing.

- He also said that the **Son of Man** had **authority** to forgive sins.

- Jesus told the man to **pick up his mat** and go home.

- Everyone was **amazed**.

Key ideas

- In the first century, some **illnesses** were considered to be punishment by God for **sin**.

- Jesus cured the paralysed man because of the **faith** of the **four friends**.

- **Blasphemy** is when a person sets themselves up to be equal with God.

- Jesus was accused by the lawyers of blasphemy. The **punishment for blasphemy** in Jewish Law could be the **death penalty**.

- Jesus' answer was to show his concern for the man's **body** and **soul**.

- The people were **amazed** because the **lawyers could not think of a reply** to Jesus' words.

Contemporary issues and evaluation

Read pages 121–122 on attitudes to death and pages 100–102 on science and religion when preparing this part.

Sample question

Q. Do healing miracles happen today?

Points to consider:

On the one hand... some argue that God can and does work in ways which we do not understand. There are many reported healings at **Lourdes** which doctors cannot explain.

On the other hand... others think there are better ways of explaining unusual cures. The **mind** can sometimes give people **unusual inner strength**. In many cases 'cures' turn out to be short term and it is clear there has been no miracle.

Your turn

Now try the sample questions on pages 59 and 60 yourself.

3.3 The calming of the storm

Read: Mark 4:35–41

Short questions

Q. What is faith?

A. Having an active trust in someone or in God

Q. What is a miracle?

A. An act of God which breaks the laws of physics

Summary of the story

- Jesus told his **disciples** to cross the Sea of Galilee by **boat to the other side**.

- A **storm suddenly blew** up and waves washed over the side of the boat.

- The boat was **full of water**.

- **Jesus** was **asleep** in the stern of the boat.

- The **disciples woke him** and asked him whether he cared if they were to drown.

- Jesus **rebuked the wind and waves** and told them to be quiet.

- There was a **great calm**.

- Jesus asked the **disciples** why they were **afraid** and **lacked faith**.

- The disciples were **terrified**.

- They **wondered who Jesus was** that the wind and waves obeyed him.

Key ideas

- This is a **nature miracle**. Nature miracles are often **more spectacular** than healing miracles and usually do not require faith in order for Jesus to perform them.

- Nature miracles illustrate **Jesus' divine powers** because just as God is described in Genesis 1 as creating the heavens and the earth, Jesus is able to control them.

- This power to control nature led the **disciples to ask who Jesus is** – the only answer is **God**.

- The disciples' **fear** was due to belief at that time that deep waters and storms were associated with the **powers of evil** which cause **human suffering**.

- The **contrast** is between **Jesus' complete trust** (he sleeps) **in God** and the disciples' **noisy fear**.

Contemporary issues and evaluation

Read pages 100–102 on science and religion when preparing this part.

Sample question

Q. Do nature miracles prove that Jesus is God?

Points to consider:

On the one hand... some argue that if nature miracles work by **suspending the laws of physics** then only God is capable of doing this without upsetting all the other laws of nature. If we believe Jesus was able to perform nature miracles then it follows **he must be God**.

On the other hand... others argue that nature miracles are **really stories or symbols about life**. In this story the storm represents all the suffering and evil in the world. We 'drown' when we **give up on life** and believe that no good can come out of bad things. Nature miracles are not there to prove Jesus was God but to **contrast his faith in God with our failings**.

✎ Your turn

Now try the sample questions on pages 61 and 62 yourself.

3.4 The rich young man

Read: Mark 10: 17–31

Short questions

From the official vocabulary list, questions might be asked such as:

Q. What is a disciple?

A. A follower or student

Q. What is justice?

A. Treating others fairly

Q. What does sacrifice mean?

A. Giving up something for something of greater value

Q. What is a parable?

A. A story or saying comparing the Kingdom of God with everyday human events

Summary of the story

- The man asked Jesus what he should do to **inherit eternal life.**

- **Jesus** told him to keep the **Ten Commandments.**

- The man said he had **kept** these since he was a child.

- Jesus challenged him to **sell everything** and give it to the poor.

- The man was **sad and left**. He was very rich.

- **Jesus** said to the **disciples** that **rich people** would find it **hard** to get a place in the **Kingdom of God**.

- The disciples were **amazed**.

- Jesus told them a **parable**: it would be easier for a **camel to pass through the eye** of a needle than for a rich man to enter the **Kingdom of God**.

- Peter said they had left everything to follow Jesus.

- Jesus replied everyone who had left his family and property would **receive it back a hundred times over** in the Kingdom of God.

Key ideas

- In the first century, having **great wealth** was a sign that you had been **blessed** by God.

- The **man** just **wanted Jesus to praise him** for keeping the Ten Commandments and being a good person.

- But Jesus' challenge was to **reverse** the man's religious views and ask him to **give to the poor**.

- As **God sides with the poor**, the man is being challenged to see whether he really believes in **justice**.

- Jesus' **disciples** clearly also **fail to understand** the nature of justice.

- Jesus imposes a **tough choice on his followers**: their primary aim should be to fulfil the demands of the Kingdom of God which might mean **leaving one's family**.

- The **reward** in the Kingdom of God is **justice** and **spiritual fulfilment**.

- The parable illustrates an **impossible problem**: a camel cannot fit through the eye of a needle.

Contemporary issues and evaluation

Read page 116 on Christian teaching on wealth and treatment of the poor when preparing this part.

Your turn

Now try the sample questions above yourself.

3.5 The woman and Simon the Pharisee

Read: Luke 7: 36–50

Short questions

From the official vocabulary list, questions might be asked such as:

Q. What is a parable?

A. A story or saying comparing the Kingdom of God with everyday human events

Q. What is sin?

A. Disobeying God and separating oneself from Him

Q. What does salvation mean?

A. Being saved and brought into a relationship with God

Summary of the story

- **Jesus** was having dinner with a rich **Pharisee called Simon**.
  - A **sinful woman** brought a jar of perfume.
  - As she **wept** she washed Jesus' **feet with her tears**.
  - She dried his feet with her **hair** and put **perfume** on them.
  - **Simon was amazed**. He thought that if Jesus was a prophet he would know she was a sinner.
- Jesus told Simon a parable about a moneylender and **two debtors**.
  - In the parable, one owed **500 denarii** and the other **50 denarii**.
  - The moneylender **cancelled both debts**.
- Jesus asked Simon which of the **debtors** would **love** the moneylender more.
- Simon answered the **one who had the bigger debt**.
- Jesus said that **Simon had failed** to act as the woman had.
- Simon had not given him a **kiss**, washed his feet and put perfume on them or anointed his head.
- The woman's many sins had been forgiven because **she loved him much**.
- Her faith had **saved** her.

Key ideas

- The contrast is between **Simon** who carried out his **minimum duties** as a host and the **woman's extravagant devotion** and **love**.

- The **Pharisees** were a group of **religious Jews** (but not priests) who thought you could only be good if you kept to all the laws of the Torah (Jewish Law) *and* all their **own interpretations** of those laws.

- Described as **sinful**, the woman was probably a **prostitute** and therefore unable to carry out the Jewish Law.

- The story teaches about **prejudices**. The woman is stereotyped as a bad person, although there is no evidence to suggest this is true.

- It was **traditional to wash** and anoint a **guest** if he had travelled during the heat of the day.

- The **Parable of the Two Debtors** is a reminder of Jesus' teaching in the **Lord's Prayer** to 'forgive us our debts' (trespasses) as 'we **forgive** those who are **in debt to us**'.

- **Debtors** can mean those who **owe us money** but also those who have **sinned**.

Contemporary issues and evaluation

Read pages 118–120 on prejudice and discrimination when preparing this part.

Sample question

Q. Was Simon the Pharisee a bad person?

Points to consider:

On the one hand... some argue that Simon was a **bad person** because, as a Pharisee, he would have been well educated, **known Torah** and would also know that the prophets taught that God prefers mercy to being very religious. Also Simon was **prejudiced against the woman**.

On the other hand... others argue that Simon was attempting to live up to the **high standards** set by the Pharisees. He might **rightly have thought** it was too easy for the woman, whom he thought was a sinner or prostitute, to seek Jesus' forgiveness when he had **always tried to live a good life**. Simon might be compared to the elder son in Jesus' Parable of the Lost Son.

Sample question

Q. Does religion cause prejudice and discrimination?

Points to consider:

On the one hand... some argue that if one holds a religious belief, then it follows that **not all other beliefs can be true**. It is therefore quite right to discriminate against those who **cause harm to innocent** people, or who abuse children, or who exploit the country's laws.

On the other hand... others argue that although some religious people are prejudiced against certain groups such as homosexuals, ethnic minorities and prostitutes, there are also many religious people who work hard to **overcome prejudices** and treat people for what they are and not for what they are thought to be.

Your turn

Now try the sample questions on pages 66 and 67 yourself.

3.6 The Good Samaritan

Read: Luke 10: 25–37

Short questions

From the official vocabulary list, questions might be asked such as:

Q. What is a parable?

A. A story or saying comparing the Kingdom of God with everyday human events

Summary of the story

- A **lawyer** asked Jesus, 'Teacher, what must I do to **inherit eternal life?**'.

- **Jesus** asked him what the **law** said.

- The lawyer answered that he should **love God** and **love his neighbour** as himself.

- The lawyer asked Jesus '**Who is my neighbour?**'.

- Jesus answered with a parable:
  - A man was travelling from **Jerusalem** to **Jericho**.
  - Robbers **beat** him up and left him for **dead**.
  - A **priest** saw the man and **crossed** to the other side of the road.
  - A **Levite** saw the man and **crossed** to the other side of the road.
  - A **Samaritan** took **pity** on him, fed him and bandaged his wounds.
  - He took him to an **inn** and gave **the innkeeper money** for further care of the man.

- Jesus asked the lawyer who was the **neighbour** to the man.

- The lawyer answered the one who had **mercy** on him.

- Jesus told him to go and **act** in the same way.

Key ideas

- The **traditional Jewish** answer to the question 'Who is my neighbour?' would be 'other Jews'.

- The point of the parable illustrates the **prejudices** people have about who is worthy to be considered a neighbour.

- In Jewish Law a **dead body** and blood were considered **religiously unclean**.

- The **priest** was probably on his way to the Temple and could not touch the body otherwise he would not have been allowed into the Temple.

- A **Levite** was an assistant in the Temple. Like the priest he would not be allowed to touch a dead body.

- **Neither man made any effort** to find out whether the man was dead or not.

- The **Samaritans** were **despised** by the Jews and treated as racially and socially inferior.

- The Samaritan acted **generously**, **mercifully** and out of **love**. He fulfilled the essence of the Jewish Law.

Contemporary issues and evaluation

Read pages 118–120 on prejudice and discrimination when preparing this part.

Sample question

Q. Is racism the worst form of prejudice?

Points to consider:

On the one hand... some argue that racism is the worst form of **prejudice** because racism has caused terrible **wars** and **massacres** such as the slaughter of the Tutsi by the Hutu in **Rwanda**. Racism also causes **mistrust** and **discrimination** in local communities based on false views of other people.

On the other hand... others argue that other forms of prejudice such as **sexism** can be just as destructive for society. Women make up half the world's population but still they find themselves **underpaid** by comparison with men. Women often fail to get the top jobs and are **not always taken as seriously** as men.

Sample question

Q. Were Jesus' parables the best way to teach?

Points to consider:

On the one hand... some argue that we **remember stories** much better than straight teaching. Jesus' parables used events from everyday life to **explain complex ideas about the Kingdom of God** very effectively.

On the other hand... others argue that however good Jesus' parables were, his **most important teaching** was done **without parables**. Sometimes parables can **confuse** as people **do not understand their hidden message**.

 Your turn

Now try the sample questions on pages 68 and 69 yourself.

3.7 The Lost Son

Read: Luke 15: 11–32

Short questions

From the official vocabulary list, questions might be asked such as:

Q. What is a parable?

A. A story or saying comparing the Kingdom of God with everyday human events

Q. What is sin?

A. Disobeying God and being separated from Him

Summary of the story

- A man had **two sons**.

- The **younger son** asked whether he could **have his inheritance now**.

- The younger son set off to a distant land and **spent everything** having a good time.

- When **famine** struck he went to work, looking after **pigs**.

- He was extremely **hungry**.

- He realised his father's servants were in a better state than himself.

- He decided to **return home**.

- He decided to say to his father '**I have sinned against heaven and against you**'.

- While the son was still some way off, his **father** saw him and **rushed to meet him**.

- His father told the servants to put a **ring on his son's finger**, kill the fatted calf and prepare a **feast**.

- He said that they should rejoice that his **dead son was now alive**, '**He was lost and is found**'.

- The **elder son** was **angry** and told his father that he had never been given a party like this.

- His father answered that the elder son had **continually enjoyed** everything he owned.

- He said that it was appropriate to **celebrate** the **return** of the son who had been lost and was now found.

Key ideas

- The parable is aimed at the **Pharisees** who were critical of Jesus' concern for outcasts.

- This parable is one of a series about the '**lost**' people of Israel (those who were considered to be sinners and who were rejected according to the Jewish Law).

- In the parable the **elder son** represents the **Pharisees** or all those who have kept to the law but are unable to be generous to those who have fallen short of its demands.

- The **younger son** represents the **outcasts and sinners** of society.

- **Eating with pigs** is an important idea in the parable. As pigs were considered unclean in Jewish Law, the younger son had reached an emotional and religious low.

- The younger son's **return** illustrates the need for all humans to **repent**, i.e. the realisation of one's faults.

- The **father** represents how **God's redemption** (His generosity, love and forgiveness) is for all sinners.

- The **feast** symbolises **joy** in the Kingdom of God.

Contemporary issues and evaluation

Read page 108 on aims and purpose of punishment when preparing this part.

Sample question

Q. Were Jesus' parables the best way to teach?

Points to consider:

On the one hand... some argue that we **remember stories** much better than straight teaching. Jesus' parables used events from everyday life to **explain complex ideas about the Kingdom of God** very effectively.

On the other hand... others argue that however good Jesus' parables were, his **most important teaching** was done **without parables**. Sometimes parables can **confuse** as people **do not understand their hidden message**.

Sample question

Q. Should the elder son have forgiven his younger brother?

Points to consider:

On the one hand... some argue that forgiveness is **at the heart of Jesus' teaching**, in the Lord's Prayer and in his treatment of tax collectors etc. The elder son should have been wise and **compassionate** enough to share in his father's joy and forgive his brother.

On the other hand... others argue that the elder brother was right to be **suspicious** of his brother. Having squandered all his money, he cannot just turn up and expect everything to go back to normal. Perhaps the younger son **needed to prove** just how **repentant** he was before his brother could forgive him.

 Your turn

Now try the sample questions above yourself.

3.8 The Sower

Read: Luke 8: 4–8, 11–15

Short questions

From the official vocabulary list, questions might be asked such as:

Q. What is a parable?

A. A story or saying comparing the Kingdom of God with everyday human events

Summary of the story

- Jesus told the crowd this parable:
  - A farmer sowed his **seed**.
  - Some seed fell on the **path**.
  - It was **trampled** on and eaten by **birds**.
  - Some fell on **rock**.
  - It **died** because it had **no moisture**.
  - Some fell amongst **thorns**.
  - It a **grew** a little but was then **choked**.
  - Some fell on **good soil**.
  - This seed yielded up a **hundred times** more seed than was sown.

- Jesus explained the parable to his disciples:
  - The **seed** is the **Word of God**.
  - The seed on the **path** is like people who **do not believe** because the **devil** makes them **disbelieve**.
  - The seed on the **rock** is like people who **receive** the word with **joy** but they have **no stamina** and when life gets difficult they **give up**.
  - The seed amongst the **thorns** is like people who after a while find **life's cares** and **desire for money choking** their faith.
  - The seed in the **good soil** is like those who have '**good and noble hearts**'. They persevere and flourish.

Key ideas

- The parable illustrates how **different people react** to Jesus' teaching about the Kingdom of God.

- The **Kingdom of God** is **God's presence in our lives now**, not just heaven.

- The parable teaches that the Kingdom **requires effort**; even though some people want to experience it, they give up for various reasons.

- Jesus probably told the parable to **encourage** his **disciples** when they felt they had **failed** in their preaching about God's Kingdom.

Contemporary issues and evaluation

Read page 113 on leadership and authority and pages 110–112 on Jesus' teaching on the Sermon on the Mount when preparing this part.

Sample question

Q. Is the teaching of the Parable of the Sower mostly about coping with failure?

Points to consider:

On the one hand… some argue that this parable is about coping with failure because the demands of the Kingdom of God of forgiveness, loving one's enemies, etc. are great and the parable shows how most people are **unable to live up to its expectations**. The parable is teaching Christians how to cope when they fail to convert other people to Christianity.

On the other hand… others argue that this parable is about being **optimistic**. They argue that although some people will fail to accept Christianity, there are many millions who have become Christians, and societies have been **transformed** by its message.

Sample question

Q. Does religion make unrealistic demands on people?

Points to consider:

On the one hand... some argue that religion asks people to change their lives so much that, as the Parable of the Sower illustrates, people are not willing to give **up all their money** and **material luxuries** even for spiritual rewards.

On the other hand... others argue that religion is a **discipline**, like sport or music, and although it can be tough at times, what it offers is **spiritual fulfilment**. This is no less realistic than training to be a good artist, writer, lawyer etc.

Sample question

Q. Were Jesus' parables the best way to teach?

Points to consider:

On the one hand... some argue that we **remember stories** much better than straight teaching. Jesus' parables used events from everyday life to **explain complex ideas about the Kingdom of God** very effectively.

On the other hand... others argue that however good Jesus' parables were, his **most important teaching** was done **without parables**. Sometimes parables can **confuse** as people **do not understand their hidden message**.

Your turn

Now try the sample questions on pages 73 and 74 yourself.

Group 2: Jesus' life, death and resurrection

3.9 The birth of Jesus

Read: Matthew 1:18–25

Short questions

Q. What is a miracle?

A. An act of God which breaks the laws of physics

Q. What does Messiah or Christ mean?

A. Anointed one

Summary of the story

- **Mary** was **engaged to be married** to **Joseph**.

- Before they were married Mary was found to be **pregnant through the Holy Spirit**.

- Because **Joseph was a righteous** man he wanted to **divorce Mary** quietly.

- An **angel** appeared to Joseph in a **dream** and told him to make **Mary his wife**.

- The angel also told Joseph to call his son **Jesus** because '**he will save the people from their sins**'.

- The angel's message **fulfilled the prophecy** which said a virgin will have a child which will be called **Immanuel**.

- Immanuel means '**God with us**'.

- Joseph woke up and did as God had told him.

- **Mary gave birth** to a son and he was called **Jesus**.

Key ideas

- In the first century, being **engaged** or **betrothed** was equivalent to being married today. To separate required a man to **divorce his fiancée**.

- Being betrothed did not mean Mary and Joseph were living together, so **Mary's pregnancy was shocking**.

- Joseph is **righteous** because, although he could have divorced Mary in a very public way on the grounds of **adultery**, he did not want to shame her more and so was going to divorce her as **privately as possible**.

- **Angels** were God's means of communicating directly with humans. **Dreams** were also a way in which God could make His intentions known. The combination of a dream and an angel shows how significant God's message was and the importance of Jesus' birth.

- The prophecy is from **Isaiah 7:14**. The prophecy speaks of a **young girl** having a child whose name would be **Immanuel**.

- There is much debate about whether Mary was a '**virgin**', i.e. having never had sex, or a young girl who was at the **age to be married** and who had become pregnant by another man.

- The events are being guided by the **Holy Spirit**. The Holy Spirit is God's **creative presence on earth**.

- '**Jesus**' is the Greek form of the Hebrew **Joshua** and means **God who saves people** – just as Joshua in the Old Testament saved the people by bringing them into the Promised Land.

- The significance of Joseph is that through him Jesus can trace his family line back to **King David**. Matthew wanted to show that Jesus fulfilled the prophecies (e.g. 2 Samuel 7:12–16) which told of the coming of the **Messiah** who would be a descendant of David.

Contemporary issues and evaluation

Read pages 100–102 on science and religion and pages 110–112 on Jesus' teaching on the Sermon on the Mount when preparing this part.

Sample question

Q. Was Jesus' conception a miracle?

Points to consider:

On the one hand... some argue that if by miracle we mean that God **suspends or breaks the laws of science** then this was a miracle. The importance of the miracle is to show that **Jesus was created uniquely** by God as His son in order to redeem the world of its sins.

On the other hand... others argue that a miracle does not break the laws of science but is a **special moment** when we become aware of God's presence. As Jesus' life was largely spent defending outcasts and those whom society despised, it makes sense to have made him an outcast by being conceived through an **adulterous relationship**.

Sample question

Q. Is Jesus' teaching more important than his birth?

Points to consider:

On the one hand... some argue that Jesus' teaching focused on the importance of how we treat others and our relationship with God. He taught about **sacrificing one's own selfish** needs for others. He did this by example, eventually dying on the cross. His birth and **origins are not significant**.

On the other hand... others argue that Jesus was more than a great teacher – he was **God's son**. Knowing about his birth means that we understand his **purpose and relationship with God**. If his death and resurrection are an important part of Jesus' story then we ought also to know how his life began.

Sample question

Q. Is Joseph the real hero of Jesus' birth?

Points to consider:

On the one hand... some argue that Joseph's willingness **to believe the dream was from God** and to marry Mary and bring up her son as his own indicates that he is the real hero of the story.

On the other hand... others argue that it was a much more frightening and dangerous experience for **Mary**. She was **very young** and to have found herself pregnant without ever having had sex with another man would have been bewildering. She also knew that Joseph was within his rights to divorce her. We do not hear Mary complain and her **obedience** to God's will makes her the **real hero of the story**.

✏ Your turn

Now try the sample questions on pages 76 and 77 yourself.

3.10 The temptations

Read: Luke 4: 1–13

Short questions

From the official vocabulary list, questions might be asked such as:

Q. What is temptation?

A. The desire to do something wrong

Q. What is worship?

A. Giving God praise and honour

Q. What is fasting?

A. Going without food to enable oneself to be more aware of God

Q. What is meant by the term Son of God?

A. Jesus' unique relationship with God

Summary of the story

- After his baptism Jesus was led to the **desert** by the **Spirit**.

- The **devil** tempted Jesus for **40 days**.

- He **ate nothing** for 40 days.

- The **devil tempted** him in three ways:

    1. The devil told Jesus that if he was the Son of God he could turn **stones** into **bread**.

        Jesus answered that **man does not live on bread alone**.

    2. The devil led him to a **high place** and offered him all the **kingdoms of the world** if he would **worship** him.

        Jesus answered that **only God** should be **worshipped**.

    3. The devil led him to **Jerusalem** and to **a high place** and told him that if he **jumped off** God's angels would catch him.

        Jesus answered that you must not **test** God.

- The **devil left him** and **angels** looked after him.

Key ideas

- John the Baptist's water baptism symbolised the cleansing of people's hearts and being prepared for the coming of God's kingdom. But for Jesus it also marked the moment when he felt God's very special **calling** by the **Holy Spirit**.

- Jesus' fast is a **test of his obedience** to God and a way of making clearer what his mission was to be as God's son.

- **The desert** is a reminder of **Moses'** and the Israelites' time wandering in the **wilderness for 40 years**. Moses and the Israelites were often tempted to abandon God during this time.

- Unlike Adam in the Garden of Eden, Jesus resisted selfishly eating during his time of fasting. This shows his **obedience** to God.

- The Israelites were obedient to God because God sent manna from heaven, but true obedience comes from listening to God's word.

- Moses was offered Canaan by God but here the devil offers Jesus the whole world. As **Messiah**, Jesus could have had **huge political power**.

- Jesus' reply that **only God should be worshipped** suggests that desiring worldly power is a form of **idolatry**. This is clearly forbidden in the Ten Commandments.

- The **high place** in Jerusalem is probably a tower in the Temple. This temptation is not a physical test but a test to prove Jesus' special powers as God's Messiah. In the wilderness the Israelites asked God for many miracle signs but Jesus shows that true belief in God's love does **not require external signs**.

Contemporary issues and evaluation

Read page 113 on leadership and authority, page 113 on non-religious ethics and wisdom and pages 114–115 on social justice when preparing this part.

Sample question

Q. Does power always corrupt those in positions of responsibility?

Points to consider:

On the one hand... some argue that power does corrupt because all people are **weak-willed** and power is exciting. The example of the Fall illustrates that humans are flawed and struggle to be good.

On the other hand... others argue there are some exceptional people who do keep to their promises and beliefs. **Jackie Pullinger**, for example, chose to help the outcasts in Hong Kong not for power or fame but because she felt it was her **vocation**.

Sample question

Q. Should one always obey God?

Points to consider:

On the one hand... some argue that in theory one should always obey God. If God is all powerful then what He commands must **always be for the good**. However, sometimes it takes a great deal of prayer and reflection to be certain that what we are hearing is God's call and not our own **selfish temptations**.

On the other hand... others argue that is **dangerous** to say one should always obey God because it is not always clear what God is commanding. Some terrorists think they are carrying out God's commands when clearly God would not ask anyone to kill innocent people.

Sample question

Q. Is cheating wrong if no one finds out and no one is hurt by it?

Points to consider:

On the one hand... some think that there are some moral values which are **always wrong**. Cheating makes you less reliable, it may hurt others **indirectly** and is a basic cause of injustice.

On the other hand... others argue that if no one is hurt then the **ends justify the means**. They say it is impossible to claim that there are some things which are always and absolutely wrong, so cheating is wrong only if it upsets others.

Your turn

Now try the sample questions on page 80 yourself.

3.11 The call of the disciples

Luke 5: 1–11

Short questions

From the official vocabulary list, questions might be asked such as:

Q. What is a disciple?

A. A follower or student

Q. What is a miracle?

A. An act of God which breaks the laws of physics

Q. What is sin?

A. Disobeying God and separating oneself from Him

Q. What is faith?

A. Having an active trust in someone or in God

Summary of the story

- **Jesus** was **teaching** a crowd by the **Sea of Galilee**.

- He got into **Simon Peter's boat** and asked him to row out on the water.

- He taught the **people from the boat**.

- Then he told Simon Peter to go into the **deep waters** and put down his **nets**.

- **Simon Peter** said they had **caught nothing so far**.

- He did as Jesus said and caught a **huge amount of fish**.

- The other fishermen rowed out and also filled their boat with fish.

- Simon Peter fell at Jesus' feet and said that he was **not worthy of Jesus** because he was a **sinner**.

- Jesus told him **not to be afraid**.

- He said that from now on they were to '**catch men**'.

- The fishermen **left everything** and followed Jesus.

Key ideas

- The story makes a **contrast** between the **faith of the large crowds** and **Peter's lack of faith**.

- The catch of the large number of fish is a **symbol** of the **large number of followers Jesus has**.

- Filling the boat is a **symbol** of the **Kingdom of God bringing fulfilment** and abundant joy.

- **Peter's confession** to Jesus shows that he **understands** the **symbol** of the catch of fish and that he is **not worthy of the Kingdom of God**.

- Peter's **humbleness** is just what is needed to make him a **good disciple**.

- The disciples are to **transfer** their skills as fishermen to become **disciples** and **preach**.

- Leaving their nets shows the **sacrifice** needed to become a disciple.

Contemporary issues and evaluation

Read pages 114–117 on social justice and treatment of the poor when preparing this part.

Sample question

Q. Does having faith in God mean one should never doubt His existence?

Points to consider:

On the one hand... some argue that doubt implies a **lack of faith**. If a person doubts God's existence then they are **not a true follower**. Faith in God does not require proof of His existence.

On the other hand... others argue that doubt is a sign that a person realises that they **cannot know everything**. Peter's humbleness in front of Jesus was a way of showing that faith also means having to trust in things we do not always fully understand.

Sample question

Q. Is loving one's family more important than loving God?

Points to consider:

On the one hand... some argue that religion can sometimes break up families and this can never be right. Christianity teaches the **importance of marriage and duties to parents** so it could never be the case that the love of God means leaving one's family.

On the other hand... others argue that Jesus never taught that a person should not love their family but it is important to be clear what their **ultimate values** are. As **God is all powerful** and all loving then there may be times when loving God must be more important.

Your turn

Now try the sample questions on pages 82 and 83 yourself.

3.12 Peter's declaration

Read: Mark 8: 27–33

Short questions

From the official vocabulary list, questions might be asked such as:

Q. What does the term Son of Man mean?

A. Jesus' role as the one who would suffer for others

Q. What does Messiah or Christ mean?

A. The anointed one

Q. What is a prophet?

A. A person chosen by God to speak God's message to the people

Summary of the story

- **Jesus** and his **disciples** were near **Caesarea Philippi**.

- Jesus asked the **disciples** who the people **thought he was**.

- They **answered** that some thought he was **John the Baptist**, some thought he was **Elijah** and some thought he was a **prophet**.

- Jesus asked the disciples who they thought he was.

- **Peter** said that Jesus was the **Messiah**.

- Jesus told them not to tell anyone this.

- **Jesus** said that as the **Son of Man** he would **suffer**.

- He said he would be **rejected** by the **Jewish authorities**.

- He said that he would **rise again** after **three days**.

- **Peter** told Jesus that he would **not let him do this**.

- But **Jesus** told **Peter not to tempt him**.

- Jesus said to him '**Get behind me Satan**'.

- **Peter** was thinking in **human terms** and not as God wished.

Key ideas

- There were many **Jewish ideas** about who the **Messiah** would be, but everyone imagined the Messiah would bring a time of **peace**, **compassion** and **justice**.

- **Ordinary people** thought Jesus was **very special**.

- **John the Baptist** had been killed shortly after Jesus' baptism and some thought his spirit was living on in Jesus.

- **Elijah** was the great Jewish **prophet** in the Old Testament and some hoped he would bring back **true worship of God**. Some thought his spirit was living on in Jesus.

- **Peter** believed Jesus to be the **Messiah** whose healings and teachings would bring the time of peace and compassion.

- Jesus explained that he also saw his **role as Messiah** as one who would **suffer for others**.

- Peter's reaction suggests he **cannot believe** that a **messiah** would **suffer**.

Contemporary issues and evaluation

Read page 121 on attitudes to death when preparing this part.

Sample question

Q. Was Jesus just a good man?

Points to consider:

On the one hand... some argue that the evidence supports this view because Jesus did not encourage the use of force or violence and he taught people to **love** their enemies and **help the weak**. They believe that his **miracles** and his **resurrection** are just exaggerated stories or **myths** to make him appear very special.

On the other hand... others argue that Jesus was a good man but he was also the Messiah and **Son of God**. They argue that there is no reason to make up his **miracles** or the **Resurrection** and these could only happen if God was working in Jesus in **some very special way**.

Sample question

Q. Did Jesus have to suffer as the Messiah?

Points to consider:

On the one hand... some argue that Jesus modelled his role on **Isaiah's Suffering Servant**. Jesus knew that only by suffering for others could he set an example of love and generosity. He also knew that this view of the **Messiah** was **not what people expected** and it would make it clear that he was not a political revolutionary.

On the other hand... others argue that a lot of Jesus' teaching suggests that he **did not think suffering** was part of his **mission**. **Peter** and later **Judas** were both very **surprised** when he did **suffer** and things appeared to go wrong. As **Messiah** he **probably** thought that **God would bring in the Kingdom of God before he died**. His crucifixion was not part of his original plan.

Your turn

Now try the sample questions above yourself.

3.13 The Transfiguration

Read: Mark 9: 2–13

Short questions

From the official vocabulary list, questions might be asked such as:

Q. What does Son of God mean?

A. Jesus' unique relationship with God

Q. What does the term Son of Man mean?

A. Jesus' role as the one who would suffer for others

Q. What does the word transfiguration mean?

A. A change in a person's appearance

Summary of the story

- **Jesus** took **Peter, James** and **John** up a **high mountain**.

- **Jesus** was **transfigured**.

- His **clothes** were **dazzling white**.

- **Elijah** and **Moses** appeared **talking** to Jesus.

- **Peter** suggested that they **build three shelters** for Moses, Elijah and Jesus.

- A **cloud** appeared and from it a **voice** spoke.

- The voice said 'This is my **Son** whom I love. **Listen** to him'.

- Suddenly Moses and Elijah had gone and only Jesus was there.

- On the way down Jesus told the disciples **not to tell anyone** what they had seen.

- The disciples asked Jesus why **Elijah** must first come.

- Jesus explained that **Elijah** must come first to **restore society**.

- In fact he had come.

- So now Jesus, as the **Son of Man**, would **suffer** many things.

Key ideas

- The **Transfiguration** reveals to the disciples Jesus' **divine identity** as God's son.

- Transfiguration means a **change in a person's appearance**.

- The event describes the **disciples' spiritual experience** of who Jesus is.

- In their **vision** the disciples saw Moses and Elijah: **Moses** represents the **Law** and **Elijah** represents Jewish **prophecy**.

- **Jesus** is **greater** than these two figures and therefore is the **fulfilment** of the **Law** and the **hope of the prophets**.

- It was believed that **Elijah** would come to prepare the people for the Messiah. So, if **John the Baptist fulfils Elijah's** role then **Jesus is the Messiah**.

Contemporary issues and evaluation

Read pages 100–102 on science and religion when preparing this part.

Sample question

Q. If Peter had seen Jesus revealed as the Son of God at the Transfiguration why did he later deny knowing him?

Points to consider:

On the one hand... some argue that Peter **may not have fully understood** what he experienced in the vision of the Transfiguration. Or he may have thought that, when Jesus was being interrogated by the Jewish authorities, if he was God's son **he could have easily escaped**. He was confused and therefore denied knowing him.

On the other hand... others argue that although Peter may have **understood some of the vision** it took a long time for it to make complete sense. It was probably not until the **Resurrection**, when Peter experienced the risen Jesus, that he realised that this was the same Jesus he had experienced in the Transfiguration.

Sample question

Q. Do religious experiences actually tell us anything about God?

On the one hand… some argue that a religious experience makes a **great impression** on a person and they feel they have come into direct contact with God. This means that God is not just an idea but **alive and real**. Moses experienced this at the **burning bush** and other influential people such as **St Augustine** and **John Wesley** felt that God spoke to them directly. Many people feel that they have experienced God's loving presence through **nature, music** or **art**.

On the other hand… others argue that religious experience is unreliable. The experience might just be our own **emotional response** to something. Often people claim to have experienced God when they are upset and need comforting, so it could be a form of **wish fulfilment**. Religious experiences might also be **far too general** to tell us anything specifically about God.

Your turn

Now try the sample questions on pages 87 and 88 yourself.

3.14 The Crucifixion

Read: Mark 15: 6–41

Short questions

From the official vocabulary list, questions might be asked such as:

Q. What is the Sanhedrin?

A. The Jewish ruling council

Q. What does the term Son of God mean?

A. Jesus' unique relationship with God

Q. What does atonement mean?

A. Getting back into a right relationship with God

Q. What is crucifixion?

A. The Roman death penalty of being nailed to a cross

Summary of the story

Jesus before Pilate:

- It was a custom at **Passover** to **release a prisoner**.

- The people wanted **Barabbas** to be released.

- Barabbas was a **murderer** and had led several revolts.

- **Pilate** asked whether he should **release Jesus**, 'the King of the Jews'.

- The chief **priests** stirred up the crowd to **release Barabbas**.

- **Pilate asked** what he should do with Jesus.

- The **crowd** shouted '**Crucify him!**'.

- **Pilate** asked what **crime** Jesus had done but the crowd still shouted 'Crucify him!'.

- Pilate **released Barabbas** and had **Jesus flogged**.

The soldiers mock Jesus:

- The **soldiers** led **Jesus** to the **praetorium**.

- They dressed him in a **purple robe**.

- They put a **crown of thorns** on his head.

- They called out '**Hail, King of the Jews!**'.

- They struck him and spat on him.

- They pretended to **worship** him.

- Then they put his own clothes back on and led him to be crucified.

The Crucifixion:

- The soldiers made **Simon of Cyrene** carry Jesus' cross.

- At Golgotha they offered him **drugged wine** but Jesus refused it.

- The soldiers crucified him.

- They **cast lots** for his clothes.

- The charge above Jesus' head read '**The King of the Jews**'.

- **Two robbers** were crucified with him.

- **Passers-by taunted** him, saying that if he was able to knock down the Temple and rebuild it he could also save himself from the cross.

- Members of the **Sanhedrin** mocked him, saying that although he saved others he could not save himself.

Jesus' death:

- The land was plunged into **darkness**.

- In the **afternoon** Jesus cried out 'Eloi, Eloi lama sabachthani', which means '**My God, my God why have you forsaken me?**'.

- Some thought he was **calling for Elijah**.

- One man offered him a **sponge soaked in wine vinegar** on the end of a stick.

- He wondered whether Elijah would save Jesus.

- Jesus **died** with a **loud cry**.

- The **curtain of the Temple** was torn in two.

- When the **centurion** saw how Jesus had died he said, '**Surely this man was the Son of God**'.

- **Women** who had followed from Galilee watched along with many other women from Jerusalem.

Key ideas

- It is **not clear** why the **Jewish authorities**, the **Sanhedrin**, wanted Jesus **dead**.

- It might have been that **Jesus** was **popular** and they feared they might **lose their authority** or that they thought he was **blasphemous** by making himself equal with God.

- **Pilate** and the **Roman authorities** might have thought that as Jesus claimed to be a king or messiah that this was **treason** against **Caesar** and he should die.

- **Pilate** might have been **weak-willed** and just wanted to keep the crowds quiet.

- Jesus' death was a **sacrifice** for human **sin**. As the suffering servant (the Son of Man), his death was an offering to God as a '**ransom**' to bring people back to God.

- Jesus' death was therefore an **atonement**; making humans at one with God.

- The ransom was symbolised by the tearing of the **Temple curtain** in two which showed that the **barrier between God and humans** was now **removed**.

Contemporary issues and evaluation

Read pages 106–107 on law and rules when preparing this part.

Sample question

Q. Was Pilate to blame for Jesus' death?

Points to consider:

On the one hand... some argue that, as governor of Judea at the time, Pilate could have dismissed the Sanhedrin's charges. He could see that **Jesus was not really a king** and was no threat to the Romans. Pilate is to blame because he was **weak-willed** and should have acted fairly.

On the other hand... others argue that Pilate was aware that, at Passover time, Jerusalem was packed with pilgrims and that if he made the wrong decision he could have had a bloody **riot on his hands**. He may have thought Jesus was innocent but it was more important to **keep the peace**. It was the **Sanhedrin that was to blame**.

Sample question

Q. Was it really necessary for Jesus to die?

Points to consider:

On the one hand... some argue that in an imperfect world the sacrifice of some for others makes it possible for life to carry on. This is what happened in the story of the *Miracle on the River Kwai* when a **soldier gave up his life to save hundreds of others from being executed**. Jesus' death was also a sacrifice.

On the other hand... others argue that Jesus did not intend to die and that his **teaching** and **healings** were easily **sufficient** to make his message about God's Kingdom clear. His **death** was **unfortunate** but **not necessary**.

 Your turn

Now try the sample questions above yourself.

3.15 The burial

Read: Mark 15: 41–47

Short questions

From the official vocabulary list, questions might be asked such as:

Q. What is the Sabbath?

A. The Jewish day of rest

Q. What is crucifixion?

A. The Roman death penalty of being nailed to a cross

Q. What is faith?

A. An active trust in someone or in God

Summary of the story

- It was the day when the **Sabbath** was being prepared.

- **Joseph of Arimathea**, a member of the Sanhedrin, asked Pilate for **Jesus' body**.

- Pilate was surprised that Jesus was already dead.

- **Pilate** asked the **centurion** to check if Jesus was really **dead**.

- Pilate gave Jesus' body to Joseph who wrapped it in a **linen** cloth.

- Joseph placed the body in a **rock tomb**.

- He **rolled a stone** across the entrance.

- **Mary Magdalene** and **Mary the mother of Joses saw** where Jesus was buried.

Key ideas

- The burial took place **quickly** on Friday afternoon **before the Sabbath.** The Jewish Sabbath rules mean that no work can be done on the Sabbath, which includes a burial.

- **Joseph of Arimathea's** presence shows that **not all** the **Sanhedrin condemned** Jesus.

- By burying Jesus in his tomb, Joseph showed his great **respect** for Jesus.

- The **stone** across the entrance is an important detail as it stresses that **Jesus was fully dead** and couldn't have revived and walked out. The Resurrection is therefore about the **transformation of Jesus' body**.

- The **two women were witnesses** to the fact that Jesus' body was **buried** and **not stolen** or **mislaid**.

Contemporary issues and evaluation

Read pages 121–122 on attitudes to death when preparing this part.

Sample question

Q. Do the women show greater faith in Jesus than his male disciples?

Points to consider:

On the one hand... some argue that as **Peter denied** Jesus and **Judas betrayed** him and the **others had fled** that they did not show **complete faith** in Jesus. The **women** had **followed** Jesus from Galilee and without fuss had **supported** him right up to his burial.

On the other hand... others argue that the male **disciples** had more **risky roles**. No one would have taken much notice of the women but the men might easily have been **imprisoned or killed on the same charges as Jesus**. Their loss of faith was only brief, as they came to Jesus' tomb later.

Sample question

Q. Is it not more likely that Jesus' body was stolen, not resurrected?

Points to consider:

On the one hand... some argue that it makes more sense to say that Jesus' body was stolen, either by his own followers because **they wanted to bury him in Galilee**, or by the authorities who were worried that Jesus' followers might turn the tomb into a **sacred site for worship**. There is a gap between the two women's witnessing of the burial and their return early the next day. The body could have been stolen by **tomb robbers** hoping to find Jesus' jewellery or money.

On the other hand... others argue that the rock across the entrance **would have been sealed shut** and, as Matthew's Gospel records, there was a Roman guard round the site. There would have been very little to gain by stealing the body and although resurrection is out of the ordinary many felt they **experienced the resurrected Jesus**.

Q. Does it make any sense to believe in life after death?

Points to consider:

On the one hand... some argue that Jesus' first disciples had **very powerful experiences** of meeting the resurrected Jesus. Paul's teaching of having **spiritual bodies** is reasonable and it makes sense that God would **reward good people** who may have suffered in this life and punish bad people who have escaped punishment.

On the other hand... **nihilists** argue that there is **no proof** for life after death and when one dies that is the end. It makes much more sense to say that we live on in the **memories of others** because it is very unclear what St Paul's spiritual body would be like.

Sample question

Q. Is it not always wrong to kill another human being?

On the one hand... some argue that if **all life is sacred** then only God should take away a life. They believe that absolute pacifism is right in saying that **all wars are unnecessary** and we can find other ways of solving disputes. It is also wrong to deliberately end another person's life, even if they are very sick, because drugs and hospices **provide good alternatives**.

On the other hand... others think that wars are sometimes necessary because we only have a duty to **protect innocent** human life not all human life. The just war argument balances protection of innocent life and using **force against evil people**. Euthanasia is not wrong because **keeping a very sick person alive is cruel**.

 Your turn

Now try the sample questions on pages 93 and 94 yourself.

3.16 The Resurrection

John 20: 1–29

Short questions

From the official vocabulary list, questions might be asked such as:

Q. What does resurrection mean?

A. Rising to new life from the dead

Q. What does the term Son of God mean?

A. Jesus' unique relationship with God

Summary of the story

The empty tomb:

- Very **early** on the first day of the week **Mary Magdalene** came to Jesus' tomb.

- She saw the **stone** had been **moved** and ran to tell **Peter** and the **Beloved Disciple**.

- Peter and the Beloved Disciple **came** to the tomb.

- When Peter looked in he saw the **linen cloths** lying there **neatly**.

- The Beloved Disciple looked in and **believed**.

Mary Magdalene and Jesus:

- **Mary Magdalene** stood by the tomb **weeping**.

- She saw **two angels** in the tomb standing at the head and feet of where Jesus had lain.

- They asked her **why she was weeping**.

- She said because they had taken her **Lord away**.

- She turned round and **saw Jesus** but **did not recognise him**.

- He asked her why she was weeping.

- As she thought he was the **gardener**, she asked him where the body had been put.

- He said '**Mary**'.

- She said '**Rabboni**' and tried to **hold** him.

- Jesus told her **not to touch** him because he had not yet returned to his Father.

- **Mary returned** to the **disciples** to tell them that she had **seen the Lord**.

Jesus appears to his disciples:

- On the **first day of the week** Jesus appeared to the **disciples**.

- They were **eating** a meal **behind locked doors**.

- Jesus said to them '**Peace be with you**'.

- He showed them the **marks** of the **Crucifixion**.

- Jesus said he was **sending them to preach**.

- He **breathed** on them as a sign of the giving of the **Holy Spirit**.

- He gave them **authority to forgive sins**.

Jesus appears to Thomas:

- **Thomas** had not been with the disciples.

- He said he would **not believe** unless he had seen Jesus' marks of crucifixion.

- A week later Jesus **passed through** the **locked doors**.

- He told Thomas to put his **finger in the marks on his hands and side**.

- Thomas said '**My Lord and My God**'.

- Jesus said that those who **believed without seeing were also blessed**.

- Jesus continued to **perform more miracles**.

Key ideas

- The **Resurrection** means that after Jesus' death he was brought back to life, not as a ghost but in some kind of **spiritual body**.

- The Resurrection was **experienced** in very **different** ways by each set of people in the story.

- **Women** had a **key role** in the Resurrection story. This shows the revolutionary teaching of Jesus because in Judaism women could not become disciples or teach.

- **Peter and the Beloved Disciple** believed in the Resurrection based on the **absence** of Jesus' body.

- **Mary Magdalene** was the **first** to 'see' the resurrected Jesus. She may **not have recognised him** because she **was not expecting to see him** or because he was **not physically the same**.

- Mary Magdalene had led a sinful life before meeting Jesus early on in his ministry.

- Mary Magdalene was told **not to touch Jesus** because she had to **learn** to **believe** in the Resurrection without having the physical presence of Jesus to depend on.

- Jesus **breathed on the disciples** as a sign that the **Holy Spirit would continue his work** in their hearts.

- **Luke** describes the coming of the Holy Spirit at **Pentecost** in a slightly different way in Acts 2 (the disciples experienced a great wind and tongues of fire), but the meaning is the same.

- The story of **Thomas** teaches that Jesus **was not a ghost** and that belief has to be based on **experiencing God's love** not on physical proof.

Contemporary issues and evaluation

Read pages 121–122 on attitudes to death when preparing this part.

Sample question

Q. Is there any evidence for life after death?

Points to consider:

On the one hand... some argue that humans are **more than** just **bodies** – our personalities indicate that we have souls. **No one** was **expecting** Jesus to be **resurrected** but **he was**, which provides evidence that our souls have some kind of existence after death.

On the other hand... others argue that there is no hard evidence for life after death – when a person dies their **body rots** and that is the end. Anything else is just **wishful thinking** and an attempt to make us feel better.

Sample question

Q. Does belief in Jesus' resurrection require evidence?

Points to consider:

On the one hand... some argue that **Thomas** was allowed to touch the wounds of Jesus in order to be convinced that the Resurrection was real and that Jesus was not a figment of his imagination. Today people find evidence such as the **Turin Shroud** and other **paranormal** experiences useful in supporting the idea of the Resurrection.

On the other hand... others argue that the main evidence comes from the **long line of Christians** who have passed on their experience of the Resurrection to one another. Jesus **blesses those who believe without seeing**. Belief in the Resurrection makes sense because it gives us a view of life as being part of a **journey** which continues on after death.

Your turn

Now try the sample questions on pages 97 and 98 yourself.

Summary

You should now know the main points and ideas behind the following:

Group 1 texts:

1. The story of Zacchaeus
2. The healing of the paralysed man
3. The calming of the storm
4. The story of the rich young man
5. The story of the woman and Simon the Pharisee
6. The Parable of the Good Samaritan
7. The Parable of the Lost Son
8. The Parable of the Sower

Group 2 texts:

9. Jesus' birth
10. The temptations of Jesus
11. The call of the disciples
12. Peter's declaration
13. The Transfiguration

14. Jesus' crucifixion

15. Jesus' burial

16. The Resurrection

You should also know the main contemporary issues relating to each of these stories.

Test yourself

Before moving on to the next chapter, make sure you can answer the following questions. Sample answers are given on pages 195–198.

Group 1 texts
1. The rich young man

(a) What does sacrifice mean? (2)

(b) Outline the story of the rich young man. (6)

(c) Explain what this story teaches about wealth and discipleship. (6)

(d) 'No one should have great wealth.' Do you agree? Give reasons to support your answer. (7)

2. The Parable of the Sower

(a) What is the meaning of the term parable? (2)

(b) Outline the Parable of the Sower. (6)

(c) Explain why Jesus told this parable. (6)

(d) 'Most people do not have strong beliefs.' Do you agree? Give reasons to support your answer. (7)

Group 2 texts
3. Peter's declaration

(a) What does the title Son of Man mean? (2)

(b) Describe the conversation between Jesus and his disciples at Caesarea Philippi. (6)

(c) Explain what this event teaches about Jesus' role as the Messiah. (6)

(d) 'Jesus was no more than just a good man.' Do you agree? Give reasons to support your answer. (7)

4. The Resurrection

(a) What does Son of God mean? (2)

(b) Describe the time when Jesus appeared to Thomas. (6)

(c) Explain what the story of Thomas teaches about belief. (6)

(d) 'If a person is religious they should have no doubts about their beliefs.' Do you agree? Give reasons to support your answer. (7)

Chapter 4: Contemporary issues

Chapters 4–10 cover Section 3 of the examination called 'World Religions and Contemporary Issues'. You only need to revise a minimum of **one** of these chapters for examination. If you are not sure which one to revise, then check with your teacher.

You can also use this chapter when revising part (d) questions in Sections 1 and 2. The ideas here will help you form your arguments.

4.1 Science and religion

For some people there is a conflict between science and religion. For others, however, there is no real conflict because scientists are not looking for meaning about the universe but answers to the question 'How does it work?' whereas religion asks the questions 'Why?' and 'What does it mean?'.

Evolution

- **Evolutionary** views are sometimes called **Darwinism** after **Charles Darwin** popularised the idea in the 19th century.

- **Evolution** is the theory that animal and plant life forms have developed and adapted from simpler forms of life.

- **Richard Dawkins** is a modern Darwinist. He believes that:
    - Religion is not only wrong but **dangerous**.
    - Religious ideas are **wrong** because they **cannot be tested** and are no more than guesswork based on the Bible.
    - Religious ideas are **dangerous** because they **brainwash children** into believing things which can cause them to become unnecessarily guilty or confused.
    - Only **atheism offers a rational view of the world**. As a biologist he thinks there is overwhelming evidence for evolution.
    - Evolution does not need God because the **world has no ultimate purpose**, but is '**blind**' or meaningless.

The universe and the Big Bang Theory

Stephen Hawkins is a modern **cosmologist** – someone who studies the origins of the universe. He believes that:

- We have enough convincing evidence to argue that the universe began **15 billion years** ago in an event called the **Big Bang**.

- We can explain the physical conditions which led to the Big Bang and these **do not rely on God**.

Creationism

Creationists believe that:

- The **Bible is directly inspired** by God through the **Holy Spirit**.

- The Bible witness is of **greater authority** than a **human scientific** view of the world.

- When it comes to understanding the origins of the universe, the **Bible offers a more accurate** account than science.

- The Bible **does not support** the scientific view of the origins of the universe because **Genesis 1** says that **God created** everything **from nothing**.

- The universe was **not created by chance**.

- Genesis says that everything has a purpose; it is **not 'blind'**.

Some creationists:

- Calculate the date of the creation from the Bible to be **4004 BC**.

- **Reject** the cosmologists' view that the Earth is 15 billion years old.

- **Reject evolution** because they argue that human beings were specially created in the image of God, and are not the **random product** of evolution.

- Believe there is **no convincing evidence** to show that humans **evolved** from lower life forms.

Some creationists support **intelligent design**, which says that:

- Many aspects of science **do support the biblical view** of creation because science often points to the **amazing complexity of creation**.

- For example, the **eye is far too complex** merely to be the product of chance – it allows us to see the world in three dimensions and in colour.

- Complexity shows us there must be a **higher intelligence** which we call God.

God and science

Progressive Christians argue that science and religion **complement** each other and there is **no conflict**. The complementary view says:

- Science offers us great insight into **how** the universe works.

- Science may **change its views** over time but there appear to be **laws of science which govern every aspect** of the universe.

- These **laws work** because **God sustains** them.

- Therefore the universe **does not collapse** into chaos.

- **Genesis is not to be read literally** but as a **poetic story** which supports the view that God is the all powerful force of the universe.

- The **Genesis** story explains **why the world is purposeful**.

- Evolution does not contradict religion because Genesis already suggests that creation is a **process**.

- Humans can still have a **special relationship with God** even if they **evolved from lower life forms**.

4.2 Stewardship and the environment

Environmental crisis

The late 20th century was a time of increasing awareness that the Earth and our way of life were being threatened by environmental crisis. The crisis is not seen as a local problem but as a concern for all people.

- The use of fossil fuels and deforestation are adding to the greenhouse gases in the atmosphere and contributing to **climate change**.

- CFCs (from fridges etc.) are depleting the **ozone layer**. This layer protects us from dangerous rays from the sun.

- The use of **fossil or natural fuels** causes pollution. These fuels will run out soon, causing a crisis.

- The rise in **world population** increases industrial processes and their effects, **pollution** due to **nuclear waste** and **land degradation** through intensive farming.

Christian teaching

There are **four Christian** principles which guide views about the environment:

- The **creation is good** because God created every aspect of it to be fruitful.

- **Humans are to be God's stewards** of creation. Being a steward means acting on God's behalf and keeping it in good order.

- The **covenant** God made with humans means that, in return for looking after the creation, God will bless and love humans.

- Once humans have **repaired the damage** done to the world because of our sinful natures, God will **restore** the world to the way it was in Eden (Genesis 2).

Conservation

Conservation means the management, protection and care of natural resources from damage and loss. This can be achieved in a number of ways:

- Through **political** means such as world earth summits. The **Kyoto Summit** (1997) set targets to lower gas emissions by implementing incentives or 'carbon credits'.

- **Thinking green** by **recycling waste**, reducing **fuel consumption** and using **alternative forms** of power.

- **Educating** people to improve their understanding of the world and the effects of their actions.

- **Protecting** children, women and racial minorities against exploitation by **multinational corporations** (MNCs) that use them as **cheap labour**.

The treatment of animals

There are two reasons why some humans treat animals differently from themselves:

- Animals are **not conscious** in the same way as humans are. Animals lack souls and therefore do not **feel pain** in the way humans do.

- Animals **do not make moral decisions** and therefore cannot be held responsible for their actions. Animals cannot have rights because rights imply responsibilities.

These two ideas have been applied to the treatment of animals in many ways. These include using animals in the following ways:

- as **food** – the **Bible does not prohibit meat eating**

- to **try out drugs** or cosmetics – humans have a more significant place on the planet

- as **organ and tissue donors** for humans – there is often a great shortage of human organs

- for **entertainment** (in circuses and as pets in the home) – they **give humans pleasure**.

Many people think that we should rethink the principles of how we treat animals. They argue that:

- We should always **avoid causing unnecessary suffering** to others. **Animals feel pain**, so as we do not *need* to eat meat to live healthy lives, we should be vegetarians.

- When God commands humans to rule the world, He means that they should use their power to **care** for it and **keep it as God intended**.

- In **Genesis 2** it is implied that **humans were vegetarian** and lived with animals without each fearing or causing harm to the other.

- Our **Christian duty is to protect** and look after animals – this should mean no animal experimentation and only having pets if they are treated with respect and dignity.

The work of A Rocha

A Rocha was started in Portugal. The name of this organisation is taken from its first field research centre in Portugal, called 'a rocha' or '**the Rock**'. A Rocha states that in all the countries where it works it is committed to **five core principles**:

- **Christian** belief in God who made the world and entrusts it to the care of human society

- **conservation** through **restoration** of the natural world by running **environmental education** programmes

- **community** as a commitment to God, each other and the wider creation

- **cross-cultural** links drawing on the insights and skills of people from diverse cultures

- **co-operation** through **partnerships** with organisations and individuals who share concerns for a sustainable world.

Their practical projects in the UK include:

- the **Living Waterways in Southall**, west London, in partnership with the local community

- supporting **churches** in recapturing the original vision of God's Earth

- the **'Living Lightly' project**, helping Christians in their everyday lives to be good stewards by making informed decisions.

4.3 Human rights, law and rules

Human rights

- Human rights can be seen as a way of protecting individual freedom against the state.

- **John Locke** (1632–1704) developed the idea of human rights to maintain **human dignity**.

- He said all human beings should be entitled to the right to **life, freedom and the pursuit of happiness**.

- **Thomas Jefferson** (1734–1826) enshrined human rights in the **American constitution**.

- Jefferson and Locke both argued that these rights are **part of nature**. This means that rights **apply to everyone** and **cannot be taken away**.

- After the atrocities of World War Two when the Nazis exterminated 6 million Jews, homosexuals and gypsies, the **United Nations** drew up a list of human rights to which it encouraged all nations to subscribe (the Universal Declaration of Human Rights).

- Human rights also imply **responsibilities – respecting the rights of others**.

Martin Luther King

- King was an **American Christian minister**.

- He planned an academic career but was persuaded to lead **a civil rights campaign** to give black African Americans **equal rights** to those of white people.

- Even though **slavery was abolished in 1865**, the southern states of America had got round this by treating black people as being 'equal but different'.

- This meant that black Americans had to create **their own schools, universities, churches**, etc.

- King argued that this was fundamentally against Christian teaching because all people are made in **the image of God**.

- He said the situation was just like that described in the Old Testament by **Amos and Isaiah** where the marginalised were being **deprived of God's justice and love**.

- He argued that the treatment of black people in American (in a Christian country) was **unconstitutional and illegal**.

- He encouraged **non-violent protest** and said that the campaigners should **treat their enemies with love not hate**.

- He led **peaceful protests** such as the **bus boycott** (1956) and the **march on Washington** (1963) where he gave his famous 'I have a dream' speech.

- In **1965** black Americans were given the **same voting rights** as white Americans.

- King was **assassinated in 1968**.

- He compared himself to **Moses** in that he knew that he wouldn't see the **promised land**, but that God would lead others to redeem America and make it a place of equality.

Children's rights

The United Nations' Universal Declaration of Human Rights gives particular rights to certain members of society. Children have certain rights because they are more vulnerable than adults and, while they are growing up, they need special protection and nurture in order to develop into healthy adults.

- **The United Nation's Convention on the Rights of the Child** was established in 1989 to protect children up to the age of 18.

- The basic children's rights include a right to:

  - **survival**

  - **protection** from harmful influences, abuse and exploitation

  - **family**, cultural and social life.

- The United Nations Children's Fund (**UNICEF**) was created in 1946 to provide healthcare for children in countries devastated by World War Two.

- UNICEF is the **only organisation** mentioned in the UN Convention on the Rights of the Child.

- The motto of UNICEF UK is '**Denying child rights is wrong. Put it right**'.

Jesus' teaching supports children's rights because:

- In his **Parable of the Sheep and the Goats** he said 'whatever you did for one of the least of these brothers of mine, you did for me'.

- In a time when children were not considered to have any rights, **Jesus chose children** as examples of what a good disciple should be.

- **He told his disciples off** when they tried to stop children from meeting him.

Law and rules

- **Laws** are laid down by **the state or monarch** and are used to help govern the country.

- Laws are enforced through **punishment**.

- **Rules act as general guidance**.

- A rule may be something which **governs a community** and which people voluntarily accept and abide by because they want to be part of that group.

- The **Rule of St Benedict** is the set of guidelines St Benedict established for his monks. These rules set out when the monks should **pray**, how they should **speak** to each other and what they should **wear**.

- Rules are **basic principles which govern laws**. For example, a rule might be that to live in civilised society we should obey the laws of the government. This is referred to as the **rule of law**.

Some **utilitarians** argue that rules are good because they promote the **greatest happiness of the greatest number** by:

- saving time

- treating people and situations in the same way and therefore maintain **fairness**

- dealing efficiently with **long-term consequences**.

The Ten Commandments

The Decalogue or Ten Commandments set up the main principles of ancient Israel as basic rules which God commanded as part of His **covenant** made with Moses.

- The principles of the Ten Commandments cover **religious** and **non-religious** life in the **community**.

- The commandments are divided into **two tablets**.

- **The First Tablet** (commandments 1–4) covers **religious rules**.

- **The Second Tablet** (commandments 5–10) covers **social, non-religious rules**.

In today's world people often say that there are **no moral absolutes** because everyone believes in different values. This is called **moral relativism**.

- The **Decalogue**, and therefore Jewish and Christian ethics, **rejects moral relativism**. For example, if it is wrong to steal, this is true wherever and in whatever period of history one lives.

However, situations can often be very complicated and sometimes it is not clear whether keeping to a particular commandment absolutely would be the better thing to do:

- Some argue that the commandments are not absolute but **guidelines**.

- Some Christians argue that they should be interpreted using Jesus' teaching of **agape** (the Greek word for **love**).

- Love means being **generous** and treating other people **as people and not as a means to an end**.

- In his **Sermon on the Mount** Jesus taught there is an **inner law of love** which should guide us.

- For example, although the rule is that murder is morally wrong, its **intentions** such as hating others are also morally very bad.

Rules and morals

Being moral does not necessarily mean one has to be a Christian.

- A person can live by general rules such as the **golden rule** which is to treat others as you would wish them to treat you.

- A person might live by the **utilitarian rule** that one should never do things to others which cause them direct pain or suffering.

- From these general rules people might then create specific rules.

- **Martin Luther King** said that an **unjust law is no law at all**. He said he was prepared to go to prison rather obey an irrational law based on prejudice.

- A rule might be broken if it means keeping to a **more important one**.

- A rule might be broken **if it causes more harm than good**.

- Some Christians argue that rules should never be broken.

- Some Christians argue that a rule may be broken out of **love** or **agape**.

Rights and punishment

- **Punishment** poses a **problem for human rights**.

- If rights are **universal** and cannot be taken away, how can the **state remove people's freedom** and restrict their happiness?

- Perhaps criminals **give up some of their rights** when they abuse the rights of others.

- There is much debate as to **which rights prisoners should lose**.

- Some argue that **prisoners** should still have a **right to vote**.

Aims and purpose of punishment

The aims of punishment serve several purposes:

- **Retribution** pays criminals back for the harm they have caused to others.
  - In the Old Testament this is called the **lex talionis** or the law of the tooth, from the phrase 'an eye for an eye, a tooth for a tooth'.

- **Protection** removes criminals from the position in which they can commit more offences by placing them in prison.

- **Deterrence** puts offenders off reoffending and stops others from committing crimes.
  - Examples are: fines, community service, imprisonment and the death penalty.

- **Reform** helps offenders to see the **error of their ways** and become responsible members of society.

- **Reparation** helps offenders understand the **effects of their crime** on the victim.
  - The offenders **repair** the damage they have done, sometimes by meeting the person they have harmed and apologising.

Prison

The purpose of prison as punishment can be for all the reasons set out above.

Prison works because:

- it reduces freedoms and rights

- if prisoners are treated with respect they may wish to reform.

Prisons may fail for a number of reasons:

- They can become **universities of crime** – prisoners can learn bad ways from each other.

- They do not do enough to **deter reoffenders**. Too many offenders on release from prison reoffend and return to prison.

- Prisons are **too full** and are understaffed. There are not enough social workers and prison officers to help in the process of reform and **rehabilitation**.

- Prisons fail to put into practice Christian teaching on **forgiveness and repentance**. In the Old Testament, **David** condemned his own adultery with Bathsheba but was allowed by **Nathan** to **make amends** rather than be punished with death.

- Prisons **depersonalise offenders**. Jesus mixed with people who had committed many offences, but he treated them as people and encouraged them to start again.

- Prisons are **not harsh enough**. Some argue that for very bad crimes prisons are too soft and do not punish enough.

Prison reform

The **Prison Reform Trust** (PRT) is a prison reform group which seeks to make prisons 'just, humane and effective'. It argues that:

- Britain has the **highest prison population** per head in Europe (151 per 100,000 of the population).

- Prison should therefore be a **place of last resort** for 'serious and violent offenders'.

- They believe: 'The Prison Service should provide **constructive regimes** in decent, safe conditions which ensure the well-being of prisoners and prepare them for resettlement in the community'.

- **Alternatives to prison** should include: fines, community service, electronic tagging, suspended sentences.

The death penalty

Some people argue that when a person commits a terrible crime they have behaved so badly that they are no longer entitled to the most basic human rights. As with a dangerous animal it is appropriate to put them to death.

Arguments for the death penalty:

- It has a strong **deterrent effect** and reduces the number of violent crimes.

- Families of victims **feel justice has been done** and it helps them come to terms with their loss.

- Some Christians argue that the sixth commandment (do not murder) does not include the death penalty, as the Old Testament sets out many crimes where the punishment is execution for **'blood guiltiness'**.

- Jesus says that 'he who **uses the sword shall die by the sword**', meaning he who unlawfully kills another must be killed.

Arguments against the death penalty:

- Jesus, in the Sermon on the Mount, says that the 'eye for an eye' law is wrong and Christians should love their enemies.

- The death penalty does not give any opportunity for repentance or forgiveness.

- It is not our place to judge whether a person should live or die but only God's. God is the ultimate judge.

- It is inhumane to kill in cold blood.

- The death penalty reduces society to the same level as the criminal.

4.4 Leadership and wisdom

From Plato and Aristotle and via Christianity, the basis for morality has always been wisdom. Being wise, however, is not just the ability to make informed decisions with skill but is also about becoming a good person.

Conscience, reason and morality

- When people talk of a good leader it is assumed that there is agreement as to what 'good' means.

- For some Christians, being good means only following the commands of the Bible.

- For others it means using one's reason to do what is right according to the general principles of Christianity.

- For others it means acting according to our conscience, which is our God-given means of knowing what God wills.

- Christians are guided in wisdom by the examples of Jesus and other Christians and by the teaching of the Church.

- Atheists argue that a person can still be good or wise without God and that being good means living according to the golden rule (to treat others as you would wish them to treat you) and with respect for others.

Jesus' teaching in the Sermon on the Mount

In the Sermon on the Mount (Luke 6: 17–49) Jesus sets out the principles of Christian morality. The sermon includes guidance on leadership and wisdom.

- The beatitudes or blessings are on those who live a Christian life and describe the right attitudes needed to become members of the Christian community (the Kingdom of God).

- An example of a beatitude is: 'blessed are you poor'. (Being poor can mean not being arrogant.)

110

- **The woes** are against those who do not act according to Christian principles.

- An example of a woe is: '**woe to you who laugh now**'. (Laughing means being complacent and not caring for others.)

- Central to Jesus' teaching is that Christians should **love their enemies**.

- The **golden rule** is to **do to others as you would have them do to you** and not just love those who love you or **lend** to those who you know will repay you.

- Finally Jesus teaches that we should treat our enemies with mercy '**just as your Father is merciful**'.

On the subject of **judging others**, the sermon states that, as **no one** is **entirely good**, they are **not** in a position to **judge others**. Only God can be the ultimate judge. Jesus says:

- Do not **judge** and you will not be judged.

- **Forgive** and you will be forgiven.

- Can **a blind man lead a blind man**? No they will **both fall into a hole**.

- Do not be **hypocritical**. Do not look at the **speck of dust** in your brother's eye when you have a **plank** in your own eye. Remove the plank first and then you will be able to see clearly to remove the speck.

Parable of the Tree and its Fruit

Jesus often **criticised** those who are **hypocrites** (saying one thing but doing something else). Here he teaches that his followers **must practise what they preach**.

- A **good tree** does **not** bear **bad fruit**.

- A tree is recognised by its fruit.

- You do not pick **figs** from **thorn bushes**.

- A **good person** brings out **good** things **stored in his heart**.

- A **bad person** brings out **bad** things **stored in his heart**.

Parable of the Wise and Foolish Builders

This parable demonstrates that **true faith requires effort** and long-term **commitment**.

- Real and false faith are like two builders.

- The **good builder** built his **foundations** on rock.

- When the **floods** came his house remained **firm**.

- The **foolish builder** did **not lay down** foundations.

- When the **floods** came his house **collapsed**.

- The foolish builder is like the man who hears Jesus' **words** but does **not put them into practice**.

Dietrich Bonhoeffer and conscience

Conscience has driven people to become leaders and bring about social reforms, build schools and hospitals, and become teachers and members of parliament.

- Bonhoeffer's example is important because, as a **Christian minister** and **academic**, he wrote about **conscience** and Christian ethics.

- He trained as a **Protestant pastor**.

- At that time **Hitler** was in power and the German Church thought it had a duty to support him.

- The Church even supported the **Reich Church** which combined Christian and Nazi beliefs. This included **anti-Semitic** teaching.

- Bonhoeffer was appointed as a **lecturer at an American university**, but because his fellow Germans were risking their lives by standing up against the Nazi regime, his **conscience demanded** that he return to Germany.

- He knew it would probably **result in his own death**.

- He returned home in 1939 and became a leading member of the **Confessing Church** which was a separate church deeply critical of the national church.

- He became involved in the **plot to assassinate Hitler**.

- This **tested his conscience**, as he had to decide whether it was right for a Christian to murder anyone, especially a leader.

- He was **arrested** and on 9 April 1945 was **executed**.

King Solomon and wisdom

The story of King Solomon illustrates a different quality of leadership – the ability to make decisions based on wisdom.

- Wisdom is not just about having knowledge but having the **skill** to use it appropriately at the right time and in the right way.

- Solomon used his **wisdom** when making a judgement between **two women** who were arguing about which one was the **true mother of a baby**.

- This shows that a **good leader** is not too grand to be involved in **everyday affairs**.

- Solomon's decision could not have been made had he not known about **ordinary human nature**.

- His **wisdom is God-given** because he is not motivated by power or glory but by **justice**.

Leadership and authority

- In the Sermon on the Mount Jesus says '**No good tree bears bad fruit**' which means Christian leadership depends on practising what one preaches.

- The Sermon on the Mount sets very **high standards** for leaders – they have to be '**merciful, just as your Father is merciful**'.

- **Saints and martyrs** are important because they are examples of a Christian lifestyle.

- They are a different kind of leader as they take seriously Jesus' command to '**become like a little child**' living a life of **humility** and to 'taking up one's cross', sacrificing their lives for others.

- **James and John** were criticised by Jesus because they **lacked humility**.

- Isaiah's strong message of judgement is against **false religious leaders** because of their **hypocrisy**.

Families are sources of leadership and authority because as St Paul teaches:

- **parents** are to **love** their children

- **children** are to **obey** their parents and respect their elders.

Non-religious ethics and wisdom

For non-religious leaders wisdom is acquired by:

- **listening** to others (the media, advisors etc.)

- being **consistent** and tolerant

- avoiding **hypocrisy**

- upholding the **laws of the land**.

Abuse of power

Power is a privilege and, used responsibly and within a moral framework, can bring enjoyment and satisfaction to those who have it and much good to those who benefit from a good leader.

- The **Old Testament** begins with several examples of how **power is abused**.

- **Cain's** desire for power causes him to **lie and murder**.

- In the story of Isaac, **Rebekah** uses her power as a wife to **trick Isaac** into blessing Jacob rather than Esau.

- **King David** abuses his power when he **steals Uriah's wife Bathsheba**, makes her pregnant and then has **Uriah murdered** by placing him in the thick of battle.

- After **Nathan's parable**, David realises the wrong he has done. He has to live with his conscience.

Examples of abuse of power today:

- **Harold Shipman** misused his power as a doctor to murder 15 of his elderly patients whilst pretending to help them. He committed suicide in prison in 2004.

- **Robert Maxwell** stole £400 million from his companies' pension fund leaving 32,000 people without pensions.

- **Soldiers in Iraq** were caught on camera abusing Iraqi prisoners.

- **Simulating drowning**, a practice used by the Americans in **Guantanamo Bay prison**, is considered to be torture and an abuse of human rights.

4.5 Social justice and treatment of the poor

Social justice

Social justice means **treating all people equally according to their needs**. Christians argue that:

- Social justice is based on the idea that as all humans are **created in the image of God**, no one can be considered to be **less valuable** than anyone else.

- Social justice recognises that **as humans exploit** each other there is a **need for law**.

- As people's behaviour is often to do with their **environment**, Christian social policy says that for there to be **justice** we have to change the **living conditions** and the **structures of society**.

- It would, however, be very unfair to help the poor more than others if they are just lazy.

- **William Temple** (1881–1944), a former Archbishop of Canterbury, was an influential writer and speaker on social justice as a member of the Life and Liberty Movement.

- He argued that what inspires people to seek social justice is being aware of **God's spirit** and having the vision of **God's kingdom** of equality on earth.

- Temple's ideas helped to inspire the foundations of the national **welfare state**.

There are also non-religious reasons for social justice. The atheist **Karl Marx** (1818–1883) argued:

- All humans share a **common humanity**.

- Therefore, if it is necessary for humans to have shelter, food and freedom then this must be **equally so for *all* humans**.

- **Competition is bad** because it gives more to some people than others.

- **Property** should be **owned by the state**.

Oscar Romero (1917–1980) is an example of a Christian who fought for social justice.

- Romero was born in **El Salvador**.

- He began life as a carpenter but later trained as a **Roman Catholic priest**.

- When he was 50 he was unexpectedly made **Archbishop** of **San Salvador**.

- It was a time of **political unrest** with a sharp rich–poor divide.

- Those who **sided with the poor** were branded as **communists** and dangerous by the government.

- Rich landowners considered **Romero to be on their side**; they did not think the Church should be **involved in politics**.

- When Romero's friend bishop **Rutilio Grande** was murdered for siding with the poor, **Romero changed his views**.

- He **challenged the leaders**, the police and others to **stop the murders** and exploitation of the poor.

- On 21 March 1980 whilst **celebrating mass**, and just after a sermon in which he had told soldiers not to obey orders and to stop the killing, **he was shot**.

- Romero said: 'I do not believe in death without resurrection. If they kill me, I will be **resurrected in the Salvadorian people**'.

Fair Trade

Fair Trade is an international movement which ensures that producers in poor countries are treated fairly by ensuring that:

- its producers are paid a **fair wage** which covers costs and labour and gives them a decent profit

- its producers are given **long-term contracts**

- its producers work in **decent working conditions** (not sweated labour)

- women and children are not exploited.

Over the years, the reduction in the price of chocolate has meant that the profits for farmers were so small that they were living in poverty. In Ghana the **Kuapa Kokoo Cooperative** has allowed workers to sell to Fair Trade partners in Europe and its profits have been invested in local projects.

Christian teaching on wealth and treatment of the poor

- In the story of the **rich young man**, Jesus challenges the view at that time that **being rich** was a sign of being **blessed by God**.

- Jesus tells the man that if he is really good he should be able to **give his wealth to the poor** and **become a disciple**.

- Some Christians argue that Jesus is just challenging how **wealth is used**.

- Some Christians argue that Jesus is just testing whether the man really **loves money** more than he loves God.

- Some Christians argue that Jesus is really questioning what **kind of society allows** a man to have so much money in the first place.

There is no one Christian view on wealth but there is a more uniform view about the poor. Christian teaching on **charity** is based on Jesus' teaching that love requires sacrifice, generosity and justice.

- Jesus said he came **not to be served but to serve** and to offer his life as a **sacrifice for others**.

- Sacrifice means giving up time, resources and lifestyle for those who do not have these advantages.

- **God's generosity is that He gave His only son** to the world as a sacrifice even though the world did not **deserve it**.

- Christians act generously by **helping the poor** even if they do not **always appear to deserve it**.

- **Amos and Isaiah** used the **example of the poor** to illustrate how a corrupt society can appear to be good.

- **Justice** is also part of Christian **stewardship** which means managing the **world's resources** and **distributing them to those who have most need**.

- Early Christians **practised a form of communism** to help the poor.

Mother Teresa of Calcutta

Mother Teresa of Calcutta (1910–1997) is an example of a Christian who worked with the poor.

- Mother Teresa was born in Uskub and her mother raised her as a Roman Catholic.

- She joined the **Sisters of Loreto** in **Ireland**.

- Feeling that her vocation was to work in **India**, she moved to **Darjeeling** in 1931.

- She took **vows** of **poverty, chastity, obedience and charity**.

- From the convent school in **Calcutta** where she worked, she could see the slums of the Motjhil area.

- Shocked by the slums, she took out medicine and food. She now felt her **vocation** was with the poor.

- She founded a new order of nuns, the **Missionaries of Charity**.

- She said '**prayer without action is no prayer at all**'.

- She set up a special **hospice for lepers**, schools for the poor, and a home for the dying who otherwise would have died on the streets.

- She created a home called **Nirmal Hriday** or Home of the Pure Heart for lepers.

- The Missionaries of Charity is now established throughout the world.

- In 1979 she won the **Nobel Peace Prize**.

Jackie Pullinger

Another example of a Christian who worked to achieve social justice is **Jackie Pullinger**.

- Jackie Pullinger was born in 1944 and always felt that God wanted her to be a missionary.

- While she was **studying music** at the Royal College of Music, she felt called to help the **poor in Hong Kong**.

- In 1966, aged 22 and supported by her church, she went to Hong Kong and taught music at a primary school in the Walled City.

- At that time the Walled City was ruled by a **gang called the Triads**.

- There was much poverty and drug use.

- She started a **youth club**, which the **Triads ridiculed**.

- She said 'If God had sent a man they'd have beaten him up'.

- She **gained the trust** of the young people and helped them to get off drugs.

- In 1981 she founded the **St Stephen's Society** to help **recovering drug addicts**.

4.6 Prejudice and discrimination

The meaning of prejudice and discrimination

- A prejudice is a belief based on **little or no evidence** or **without reason**.

- **Prejudices occur** because people make **generalisations** or **stereotypes**.

- When linked with **discrimination**, prejudice **causes injustice**.

- Prejudice and discrimination are **dangerous** because they are irrational and irrational people cannot be persuaded to see **why they might be wrong**.

- Together they lead to the **violation of human rights** and loss of human dignity.

Anti-prejudice and discrimination laws

Anti-prejudice laws are intended to make society a fairer place by protecting minorities and those traditionally considered to be inferior. The laws are also intended to change people's **mindset** and make it clear that prejudices are irrational and wrong.

Some people object to anti-prejudice laws because they believe:

- laws are **not there to make moral judgements**

- the role of law is to allow people **freedom to act and think as they wish**

- anti-discrimination laws **interfere too much** with an individual's freedom to believe what he or she wants.

Key anti-prejudice and discrimination laws include the:

- Sex Discrimination Act (1975)

- Race Relations Act (1976)

- Disability Discrimination Act (1995).

Racism and multi-racial societies

The Race Relations Act (1976) does not make it illegal to hold racist views but it does make it illegal to treat others less favourably because of their race.

- An example of **direct race discrimination** is when someone is refused a job because of their colour or ethnicity.

- An example of **indirect discrimination** is when a person is unable to do a job because they are not permitted to do something because of their ethnicity.

- In 2003 an amendment to the **Race Relations Amendment Act** (2000) made it illegal to discriminate on grounds of **religious belief**.

These laws recognise that Britain is a **multi-racial** and plural society. This means that laws are necessary in order that we all get on. These laws suggest that:

- Having **many beliefs and customs** is **better than having a few or one**.

- **Traditional values have to be revised** or abandoned.

- **Minorities need protecting** perhaps through 'affirmative action'.

But multi-racial aims can **cause racism** because they appear to be undermining the society in which people were brought up.

Some argue that Britain has **always been multi-racial**. They point out that:

- In the past **invaders** such as Romans, Vikings and Normans settled in Britain and intermarried.

- **Refugees** have come to Britain when they were persecuted, knowing that British society is tolerant. These include Hugenots, Jews and Eastern European political refugees.

- **Post-colonial** people have settled in Britain because, as British citizens, they had a right to do so even when Britain no longer had an empire.

- **Economic migrants** (those seeking jobs because work is more plentiful here than in their own countries, such as India, Bangladesh, Poland etc.) have settled in Britain.

Today's outcasts

Certain groups of people are marginalised in society.

- The **poor** are often considered to be **spongers**, lazy, thieves and anti-social.

- **Drug addicts** are often thought to **abuse the law**, steal, be abusive and cause others to feel threatened.

- **Disabled** people are sometimes considered to be **less human**, lacking in intelligence and unable to be part of society.

- **Women** are sometimes treated as if their **only role is to be mothers**.

Christian teaching and example

- **Jesus' teaching** and actions were targeted at the marginalised of his day.

- Jesus followed in the footsteps of the great **Old Testament prophets**.

- Amos and Isaiah in particular aimed their message at the rich leaders of Israel who had '**trampled on the poor**' and denied them justice.

- God's kingdom is where **God's spirit** is at work in **minds and hearts** transforming this world.

- Jesus' **Parable of the Good Samaritan** is about challenging prejudices against the marginalised.

Trevor Huddleston

- Trevor Huddleston (1913–1998) campaigned against **apartheid** in South Africa.

- He was influenced by the **Christian socialist movement** at university.

- He joined a very small order called the **Resurrection Fathers**. They sent him to Sophiatown near Johannesburg in 1943.

- He supported the **African National Congress** (ANC).

- He wrote *Naught for your Comfort* (1956) which accused South Africa of racism, prejudice and legalised persecution.

Meg Guillebaud

- Meg Guillebaud was brought up in **Rwanda** and in 1976 trained for ordained Christian ministry.

- Having lived in the UK, she returned to Rwanda in 1995 and was appalled by the **genocide** caused by the ethnic wars between the **Hutu** and **Tutsi** in 1994 (during which almost 1 million people were massacred and 3 million escaped the country).

- Despite the horrors, people still believed God would act to bring good out of evil.

- She felt her vocation was to help **widows and orphans** from **both tribal groups**.

- Her role in **reconciliation** was to teach sewing so that women could find an income.

- She helped those who had suffered to find their dignity and to forgive those who had wronged them.

- She developed the **ceremony of the scarf**:

  - A scarf is tied round the wrists of the **victim** and the **perpetrator** to symbolise how they are **bound to each other**.

  - The **victim** then ties their scarf to the **cross**, symbolising how their **pain is taken by Christ**.

  - The **perpetrator** then does the same to represent their **repentance** and desire to make amends.

  - Both are set free and can start life anew.

4.7 Attitudes to death

Life after death

Although Jesus did not say a great deal about life after death, his teaching suggests that his own death and resurrection were to enable humans to have a new relationship with God in heaven.

- Jesus said about heaven: 'in my Father's house there are **many rooms**... I am going to **prepare a place for you**' (John 14:2).

- In the **Book of Revelation** John the Divine says that in his vision he sees this world pass away to be replaced by a **heavenly Jerusalem** of peace reserved for the 'saints' – those whose sins have been 'washed away'.

- St Paul says that after death, in heaven, we are all given **new spiritual bodies**.

- Life after death is preceded by the **Last Judgement** at which everyone is judged according to their life on earth.

Nihilism

- Nihilists are **atheists** who do not think that the body and soul can be resurrected after death.

- They believe that when one dies that is **the end**.

- They believe that there is **nothing to fear** about death because one cannot **experience being dead**.

- **Humanist nihilists** believe that a **person lives on** after death in the **memories of others**.

Sanctity of life arguments

Christian teaching is that all human life is equally valuable because it is **God-given**. This is supported by various Bible passages.

- Genesis 1:27 states that human life is made in the image of God. Life is special and must be protected.

- **Life is a gift** which only God can take away.

- Psalm 139:13 states that life is sacred from the **moment of conception**.

- The **Ten Commandments** state that **killing an innocent life** (murder) is **morally very wrong**.

- Jesus said 'greater love has no one than this, that he **lay down his life for his friends**' (John 15:13), so dying for others is permitted.

- Some Christians argue that to die as a **martyr** or a **soldier** is an act of Christian love.

Quality of life arguments

- There are many who do not accept the sanctity of life.

- **Atheists** argue that life is **not God-given**.

- They argue that the only way to judge whether a life is worthwhile is whether a person is **free from pain** and can **do what they want**.

- Some Christians support quality of life arguments. They argue that if life is a gift from God, then there may be times when a person can decide not to live.

Euthanasia and ending life

Euthanasia means a '**good death**'. Those who support euthanasia sometimes call it **mercy killing**.

Arguments **against euthanasia** include:

- A sick person might feel they do not want be a burden and ought to die.

- If sick people are allowed to die, it might gradually lead to not very sick people being allowed to die.

- Drugs have improved people's quality of life so that they do not feel the need for euthanasia.

Arguments **for euthanasia** include:

- It is **cruel** to make someone stay alive if they are in pain.

- If people have a **right to life** then they also have a **right to die**.

- People who have a **low quality of life** such as those in **persistent vegetative states** (PVS) should be allowed to die.

Cicely Saunders and the hospice movement

- Cicely Saunders (1918–2005) worked in St Thomas's Hospital, London where she met a Polish Jew, David Tasma.

- He was dying of cancer and she visited him 25 times over two months.

- He said how much her visits meant to him.

- He left her £500 in his will and she used this to help others who were dying.

- She **retrained as a doctor** and pioneered **palliative care**.

- She opened her first **hospice, St Christopher's**, in 1967 in London.

- She was made a dame in 1980.

- She was against euthanasia and regarded it as a failure of society to help the very sick.

War and pacifism

Pacifism covers a range of attitudes.

- **Absolute pacifists** believe that there is **never any justification** for the use of violence.

- Jesus taught that we should love our enemies and forgive those who hate us.

- **Quakers** teach that all humans have the same spark of divinity, so to deliberately kill another human violates what we value in ourselves. They argue that all humans have the power to **create just and fair societies without resorting to violence**.

- **Weak pacifists** argue that violence and war should only be used as the **very last resort** to protect the weak. They argue that other **non-violent** means **must always be used first**, such as protests, civil disobedience, refusing to trade and marches.

Many weak pacifists support the **just war argument** (JWA). The JWA does not say war is good, but that it can sometimes be justified if it:

- is **authorised** by a **democratic government**

- has a **just cause** – such as defence

- **has good intentions** – to resist evil and promote good

- is **proportionate** to the good end

- is a **last resort**

- has a **reasonable chance of success**

- uses proportionate force in battle

- protects **non-combatants** (those who are not soldiers)

- **restores** law and order and the **environment** afterwards.

Christians are divided about whether they should support absolute or weak pacifism. Jesus' teaching is ambiguous.

- Some say that the **Sermon on the Mount** only sets up an **ideal** of pacifism.

- Jesus **did not condemn soldiers**.

- He did not say anything **explicitly against war**.

- He also taught that Christians should **obey the state**, so if the ruler commands that citizens should fight, then the Christian has a duty to obey.

- On the other hand, he told **Peter to put away his sword** when he was arrested at Gethsemane.

- He commended the **peacemakers**.

- As the Kingdom of God is a **state of peace**, some argue that Christians have to be **absolute pacifists**.

Summary

You should now know the following:

1. The various views about the relationship between science and religion

2. The religious and non-religious views about stewardship and the environment

3. The religious and non-religious views about human rights, laws and rules

4. The religious and non-religious views about leadership and wisdom

5. The religious and non-religious views about social justice and treatment of the poor

6. The religious and non-religious views about prejudice and discrimination

7. The religious and non-religious views about attitudes to death

Test yourself

Before moving on to the next chapter, make sure you can answer the following questions. Sample answers are given on pages 198–199.

1. Describe the views of creationists. (6)

2. Outline what Christians mean by stewardship of the environment. (6)

3. Outline the reasons for having children's rights. (6)

4. Describe how Dietrich Bonhoeffer's leadership was based on conscience. (6)

5. Outline the Christian teaching on the sanctity of life. (6)

Chapter 5: Christianity

Chapters 4–10 cover Section 3 of the examination called 'World Religions and Contemporary Issues'. You only need to revise a minimum of **one** of these chapters for examination. If you are not sure which one to revise, then check with your teacher.

> **BC** means **Before Christ**.
>
> **AD** means **Anno Domini** or the 'the year of our Lord' i.e. the year when Jesus was born.
>
> The western dating system is based on Christianity. However, you will see below that most scholars date Jesus' actual birth to be earlier than year 1.

These revision notes follow the order of JF Aylett and Kevin O'Donnell's *The Christian Experience*. You must make sure that you understand and learn the ideas in *The Christian Experience* as well as the notes below.

5.1 Jesus

Jesus is the central figure in Christianity. Although Christians consider that he lived a mortal life they also believe that he was divine.

- Jesus was born in **Bethlehem in** around **4 BC**.

- Not much is known of his early life in **Nazareth**.

- At the age of 30 he was **baptised by John the Baptist** and felt that God had **specially chosen him**.

- He lived, worked and **preached** around **Galilee**.

- He chose **12 men** as his **disciples**.

- He performed **miracles** especially **healings**.

- He **taught** about **preparing** for the **Kingdom of God**.

- His **parables** explained how **love** is more important than **keeping to religious laws**.

- His teaching often **upset** the **Jewish** and **Roman authorities**.

- He was **betrayed by Judas**, one of his disciples, **to the Jewish authorities**.

- The **Jewish** authorities **handed him over** to the **Romans**.

- Pontius **Pilate**, a Roman Governor, sentenced him to **death**.

- He was **crucified** in 29 AD.

- **Three days later** he **rose** from the dead.

- He **ascended** into **heaven** to be with God.

- Christians believe he is the **Son of God** and the **Risen Lord**.

- Christians believe his **death pays off** people's **sins**.

5.2 The Bible

The Bible is the basis on which Christians develop their central beliefs. Although parts of the Bible are very ancient, Christians believe that through study, reflection and discussion, people can use it as a sound guide for life today.

The content of the Bible

- The term **bible** means **many books**.

- The **Old Testament** contains the **Jewish scriptures** such as law, prophets, history and poetry.

- The **New Testament** contains the four Gospels, Acts of the Apostles, many letters and the Book of Revelation.

- The **Gospels** tell of **Jesus' life**, teaching, death and resurrection.

- The term **gospel** means **good news**.

The authority of the Bible

Christians believe that:

- The Bible is the **Word of God**.

- The writers of the Bible were **inspired** by God's **Holy Spirit** to write it.

- The Bible contains the **code for living**.

- The Bible contains **truth**.

Difficulties with the Bible

The Bible contains elements which are hard to understand or can be interpreted in a number of ways.

- Some of the **violent** stories in the Old Testament **clash** with **Jesus' teaching on love**.

- There are many **miracle** stories which modern people find **difficult** to believe happened.

- It is sometimes difficult to know when a story is **symbolic** or **literal**.

- It is not always clear which **laws** of the Old Testament **Jesus rejected**.

5.3 Beliefs

The **main** Christian **beliefs** are contained in the **Creed** (meaning 'belief'). The Creed is often said at a church service and is what defines a person as a Christian. The main points referred to in the Creed are:

The Trinity

- There is **one God** who exists in **three persons**.

- He is **Father**, the **creator** of all things and who is beyond us.

- He is **Son** who in **human form is Jesus Christ**, who is 'God with us'.

- He is **Holy Spirit**, who is everywhere around us and the **source of inspiration**.

The Holy Spirit

- The Holy Spirit is the **third person** of the Trinity who:
  - lives or **dwells** on earth in the **hearts of people** and in the **Church**
  - is **invisible**
  - gives **comfort**
  - inspires **prayer**
  - is the source of **truth**
  - is **symbolised** by **wind**, **dove**, **fire** and **water**
  - inspired people to write the **Bible**.

Jesus Christ

- Jesus is the **incarnation** of the **Son**, the **second** person of the **Trinity**.

- **Incarnation** means to **become human**.

- Jesus died for the **sins of the world**.

- His **resurrection** is a sign of **victory over sin and death**.

- He **ascended** to God the Father in **heaven**.

- Jesus' **death** and **resurrection** promises **eternal life** for believers.

- Jesus will **return on judgement day** to judge the living and those who have died.

Sin and forgiveness

- **Sin** is **hurting** someone, yourself or God by rejecting or ignoring them.

- All people sin.

- Sin can be **deliberate** or **unintentional**.

- As God is **love** He wishes to **forgive** us our sins.

- God sent His Son to express His **love** for the world.

- Jesus died on the **cross** for our sins so that people can be **forgiven**.

- Christians should follow Jesus' example and **forgive** others.

Life everlasting

- God will **judge** all people according to their **life on earth**.

- God will grant **life everlasting** or **life after death** to the **faithful**.

- In **heaven** the soul of the departed can **meet** with the **souls** of **family** and **friends**.

- **Heaven** is beyond time and space.

- Heaven is a **mystery**.

- Heaven is **spiritual**.

- Heaven is **eternal**.

5.4 Baptism

Baptism is a special ceremony which welcomes a person into the Church community. It is most often performed when the person is still an **infant**, though in some denominations baptisms occur when the person is older and decides to join the Church. This is called a **believer's baptism**.

Infant baptism

- An **infant** is baptised using a **font** filled with **water**.

- **Parents** and **godparents** make **promises** to bring up the child in a Christian way.

- The child is given a **Christian name**.

- **Water** is poured over the child's **head**.

- The **priest** prays that the child be **protected from evil**.

- The **sign of the cross** is made.

- In **Orthodox** churches the **sign is made with oil**. This is called **Chrismation**.

- A **lighted candle** is given to **parents** and **godparents** to remind them of their **duties** to the child.

Believer's baptism

- This usually happens for people who are **12 years and older**.

- They must **ask** for it to happen.

- They must **repent** of their sins.

- They give a '**witness**' to the congregation explaining why they wish to be a Christian.

- The **minister** holds their **head** and **hand**.

- They are **plunged** backwards fully into **water**.

Symbols used at baptism

- Baptism is the moment when a **person becomes a Christian**.

- Jesus used **water baptism** to symbolise the **end** of one's **old life** and the **beginning** of a **new** one.

- **Water** is a symbol of **life** and of **washing away sins**.

- **Oil** is a symbol of God's **Spirit**.

- The **candle** is a symbol of the **presence of Christ**, who is the light of the world.

- The **candle** also symbolises how a person passes from **darkness to light**.

5.5 Prayer

There are many reasons why people pray. It is not always to ask God for something but often to reflect on what God is and what He wants. Christians believe prayer is offered through Jesus Christ and is guided by the Holy Spirit.

How Christians might pray

Christians might:

- go to **church** to pray and worship

- use **icons** or a picture of a saint, Jesus or the Holy Family

- light a **candle**

- **kneel** as a sign of **humbleness** before God

- make the **sign of the cross**

- pray to their own particular **saint**

- use the **Lord's Prayer**, the prayer Jesus taught.

Types of prayer

There are prayers which:

- **praise** God
- **thank** God
- ask for **forgiveness**
- ask for help or guidance for **the person who is praying**
- ask for help or guidance for **others**; these are called **intercessions**.

5.6 Places of worship

The most typical place of Christian worship is a church. Traditionally churches are found at the centre of a community. Large churches where a bishop is based are called **cathedrals**. Many schools, colleges and hospitals have their own much smaller space for worship which is called a **chapel**.

Typical Anglican or Roman Catholic church

- The **altar** is at the **east** end of the **church**. A **crucifix** or **cross** is placed on it to symbolise Jesus' **death and sacrifice**.
- The **pews** or seats are in the **nave** of the church for the **congregation**.
- The **pulpit** is a raised reading desk in the **nave** for **sermons**.
- The **lectern** is a reading desk used for **reading the Bible**.
- The **font** is usually at the **west** end of the church and is used for **baptisms**.
- The **windows** depict **stories** from the Bible.
- An **organ** is used for music.
- There may be a **side chapel** dedicated to a particular **saint**.

Typical Baptist or Methodist church

- There is usually a **raised pulpit** in the **centre** of the building for **preaching** and **reading the Bible**.
- The **table** or **Lord's Table**, is in **front** of the **pulpit** and is used for **communion**.
- There is **simple decoration**.
- There tend **not** to be **pictures** in the windows etc.
- There are chairs/pews for people to sit on.
- There is sometimes an **organ** used for music.

Typical Orthodox church

- There are many **icons** or special paintings of Christ and the saints.

- The main feature is an **iconostasis**, a screen containing the icons.

- The church is lit with many **candles**.

- The **font** is usually at the **west** end of the church and is used for **baptisms**.

- Often there are **no pews** or seats – people stand.

5.7 Holy Communion

Holy Communion remembers **Jesus' last supper** with his disciples. For many Christians this is the most important act of worship each week and is the moment when they feel that, through the symbols, they come into the presence of Christ. Holy Communion is also known as **mass**, **Eucharist**, and the **Lord's Supper**. Communion can be very elaborate or very simple, but a typical service usually includes the following:

- **Hymns**/songs are sung at the start and throughout.

- There are **prayers** of **intercession**.

- Two readings from the **Bible follow**, from the **Old and New Testaments**.

- The minister gives a **sermon**.

- **Roman Catholics** and **Anglicans** come to the **altar rail**.

- The **priest** gives worshippers **bread and wine**.

- **Orthodox priests** come to the people and give them **bread/wine** on a **spoon**.

- In the **Free Churches** congregations drink wine in **small glasses** where they are **sitting**.

- **Bread** is **passed round**.

- **After communion** there are final **prayers** and the **blessing** given by the **priest** or **minister**.

5.8 Marriage

For some Christians marriage is a sacrament, a holy bond, which cannot be undone through divorce. All Christians regard it as a sign of love between a man and a woman.

A wedding ceremony

- The minister explains the **purpose of marriage**.

  - Marriage is to **one person** for the **whole of this life**.

  - Marriage is for **children** to **grow up securely**.

  - Marriage is for two people to **grow** in **love** and **companionship**.

- The bride and groom both make **three promises** to the **congregation**.
  - They promise to **love** and be **faithful** only to each other for life.
  - They promise to **honour** each other for life.
  - They promise to **protect** and look after each other for life.
- The **minister pronounces** them to be **husband and wife**.
- **Marriage symbols** might include: the **exchange of rings**, **wearing of crowns**, wearing a **white dress**, wearing a **veil**.

Divorce

- **Divorce** is only accepted in **some churches** when the **relationship has died**.
- **Roman Catholics** do **not permit divorce** but only **annulment**, which means that the marriage **never happened**.

5.9 Holy Week and Easter

Easter is the most important festival in the Christian year and marks Jesus' resurrection from death. A forty day period called Lent leads up to the week before Easter, which is called Holy Week. During this week Christians remember Jesus' last week in Jerusalem and his death on the cross.

Lent

- Lent begins on **Ash Wednesday**.
- Some Churches place **ashes** on people's foreheads as a symbol of **sorrow** for sin and mortality.
- Christians **prepare** for Holy Week and Easter during Lent.
  - They may attend **Lenten services** or take up extra **praying** or **reading of the Bible**.
  - They may **give up a luxury** and try to **resist temptation** or **fast**.
  - They remember Jesus' time in the **wilderness** when he **fasted** and **resisted temptation**.

Holy Week – Palm Sunday

- On Palm Sunday Christians remember **Jesus' entry** into **Jerusalem**.
- **Palm branches** are placed in churches and some Christians wear palm crosses.
- There are church **processions** and special **services** in church.

Holy Week – Maundy Thursday

- On Maundy Thursday Christians remember **Jesus' Last Supper** with his disciples.
- **Maundy** means **commandment**. Jesus commanded his disciples to **love one another as equals**.

- As Jesus washed his disciples' feet, many **ministers wash** the **feet** of their **congregation**.

- There are special **services** of **Holy Communion**.

- Many churches hold **special prayer services**.

Holy Week – Good Friday

- On Good Friday Christians remember Jesus' **trials** and **death** by **crucifixion**.

- Some churches have special **services** when all the **items on the altar** are **removed**.

- **Pictures** and **crosses** in the church are **covered** with **dark materials**.

Holy Week – Holy Saturday vigil

- On Holy Saturday Christians remember the moment when **Jesus** was **raised from the tomb**.

- Worshippers wait up **late** and **pray**.

- Many light **candles** and **bonfires**.

- **Light** symbolises the **hope over evil** which the Resurrection brings.

Easter Sunday

- On Easter Sunday Christians remember the moment when the **women** came to the **empty tomb**.

- People attend church for special **services**.

- The **readings** in church recall when **Mary Magdalene** and the other disciples **met** the **risen Jesus**.

- There are **joyful hymns** celebrating Jesus' **resurrection**.

- People **greet** each other with '**He is risen, Hallelujah**'.

- The church is filled with **flowers**, and **eggs** are given to children as symbols of **new life**.

5.10 Festivals

Christmas

- **Advent** is the period of **four weeks before** Christmas.

- People make **Advent wreaths** with four candles which they light each Sunday before Christmas.

- Some people have **Advent calendars** which mark the days up to Christmas Eve.

- On **Christmas day** Christians remember Jesus' **birth** and the **incarnation** of God in Christ.

- People **attend church** and listen to **readings** about Jesus' special **birth** in **Bethlehem**.

- **Prayers** remember the **poor**, the **sick** and **children in need**.

- It is a time of **giving to charities**.

- At home **presents** are exchanged.

Pentecost

- At Pentecost (also known as Whitsun) Christians remember the **coming** of the **Holy Spirit** on the **apostles** after **Jesus' ascension** into heaven.

- The **apostles** were able to speak in **different languages** and could be **understood** by all different nationalities.

- It is traditionally a time when people are **baptised** and become members of the Church.

- Pentecost is considered to be the **birth of the Church**.

Harvest

- Harvest festival is a time of **thanking God** for **creation** and the gifts of nature.

- People bring **food** to church.

- A special **harvest loaf** is baked.

- **Hymns** remember God as **creator** and **provider**.

- The **food** is **distributed** to the **poor** in the parish.

- It is a time of giving to **charities**.

5.11 Pilgrimage

Pilgrimage is the act of making a journey to a place which has special religious significance. People who make them are known as **pilgrims**.

Canterbury

- **Canterbury** is the **home** to the senior bishop or **archbishop** in the **Church of England**.

- **The Archbishop of Canterbury** is also the senior bishop of the Anglican church.

- **St Thomas à Becket** was martyred (killed for his beliefs) in Canterbury on 29 December **1170 AD**.

- **Becket** is remembered as a **saintly man** who **refused** to carry out the **orders** of **King Henry II**.

- **Miracles** were recorded at **his tomb**.

- **Canterbury** has been a very popular **pilgrimage** centre ever since.

- For example, **Chaucer's** *Canterbury Tales* contains the kind of **stories pilgrims told** on their way to Canterbury.

Walsingham

- Lady **Richeldis** had a vision of **Mary** in **1061AD**.

- In the **vision** she saw a **spring of water** which could **heal**.

- The spring was **discovered** and a special **house** was **built** over it.

- The shrine was **destroyed** in **1538 AD** but **rebuilt** in the **20th century**.

- People **today** go there to seek **healing** and **peace**.

- In addition to the **Anglican** church in Walsingham there are **Roman Catholic** and **Orthodox** churches.

Rome/the Vatican

- The **Vatican** is **home** of the **Pope**.

- The Pope is the **successor** of **St Peter**.

- **St Peter** is **buried** beneath **St Peter's Church** in the Vatican.

- **Pilgrims** often attend large **audiences** there given by the **Pope**.

- Pilgrims also **visit** other churches in Rome such as the **Basilica of St Paul**.

- They also go to the **catacombs** where **early Christians worshipped** and were **buried**.

Holy Land

- Pilgrims visit the Church of the Nativity in **Bethlehem** where **Jesus** was **born**.

- They travel to **Galilee** and visit Capernaum where **Jesus taught**.

- Pilgrims go to the **Mount of Beatitudes** where Jesus gave the **Sermon on the Mount**.

- In **Jerusalem** they follow the **route** Jesus took to his **crucifixion** called the **Via Dolorosa**.

- Pilgrims visit **Jesus' tomb** and **pray** at the **Church of the Holy Sepulchre**.

Lourdes

- In **1858** a young Roman Catholic girl **Bernadette** had visions of **Mary**.

- In her visions Mary pointed to a **spring of water** which could **heal**.

- A **spring** later appeared in a cave.

- Thousands come each year for the **healing gifts** of the water.

Summary

You should now know the following:

1. The key facts about Jesus and his life

2. The importance of the Bible

3. The main Christian beliefs outlined in the Creed

4. The significance of baptism and the different ceremonies

5. The different types of prayer and ways of praying

6. How places of worship differ depending on the denomination

7. How Holy Communion is celebrated

8. The role of marriage in Christian life

9. The main acts of worship during Holy Week and the festival of Easter

10. The main Christian festivals

11. The main pilgrimage sites and their significance

Test yourself

Before moving on to the next chapter, make sure you can answer the following questions. Sample answers are given on page 199.

1. Describe the main events of Jesus' life. (6)

2. Describe what happens at a typical Christian wedding ceremony. (6)

3. Explain why the Bible is important for Christians. (6)

4. Explain what Christians believe about God. (6)

5. Describe **one** place where Christians go on pilgrimage. (6)

Chapter 6: Judaism

Chapters 4–10 cover Section 3 of the examination 'World Religion and Contemporary Issues'. You only need to revise a minimum of **one** of these chapters for examination. If you are not sure which one to revise, then check with your teacher.

BCE means **Before the Common Era** and is equivalent to using BC.

CE means the **Common Era** and is equivalent to using AD.

In traditional Judaism dates are given from the creation of the world.

These revision notes follow the order of Liz Aylett and Kevin O'Donnell's *The Jewish Experience*. You must make sure that you understand and learn the ideas in *The Jewish Experience* as well as the notes below.

6.1 Abraham and Moses

Abraham and Moses played important parts in the origins and history of Judaism.

- **Abraham** lived around **1800 BCE** and is called the **Father of the Jews**.

- He lived as a **nomad** in **Ur** in **Mesopotamia** and **at first worshipped many gods**.

- However he **felt** the **call** of the **one God**.

- **God** told Abraham to **travel** from **Ur to Canaan**.

- God made a **covenant** with Abraham and promised him **land** and **many descendants**.

- Although Abraham and Sarah couldn't have children, **God enabled Sarah** to give birth to **Isaac**.

- God **tested Abraham's** faith by telling him to **sacrifice** Isaac.

- Abraham's **faith** was **sound** and God **renewed the covenant**.

- **Isaac** and then **Jacob** became the next **patriarchs**.

- **God changed Jacob's name** to **Israel** – the people were therefore known as **Israelites**.

- **Moses** was born in **Egypt** around **1270 BCE**.

- **Moses** tried to **persuade Pharaoh** to **free** the **Hebrew** slaves.

- **Pharaoh** was **reluctant**, so **God** sent **ten plagues** and the **Hebrews escaped** through the Red Sea.

- This event is called the **Exodus**.

- In the **Exodus** to the promised land God gave **Moses** the **Torah or Law**.

- After **Moses' death Joshua** took over, **captured Jericho** and the people **settled** in **Canaan**.

- The people were then **formed** into **12 tribes**.

6.2 Holy books

The terms **Tenach**, **Torah** and **Talmud** refer to various Jewish holy books, but they are all closely related to each other. The Tenach refers to the whole of the Hebrew Bible (which many Christians refer to as the Old Testament), of which the **Written Torah** or **Law** is a part. The **Talmud** is a separate book (in fact many books) and contains the Oral Torah. For Orthodox Jews all these books can simply be referred to as Torah.

Torah

- Torah means **teaching**.

- It is the **first five books** of the **Tenach** or Hebrew Bible.

- Torah contains **commandments** and **stories**.

- Torah is the **heart** of the **covenant** made with **Moses**.

- It contains **613 commandments** or **mitzvoth**.

- The **Ten Commandments** are the ten central mitzvoth.

- Torah is **read** in the **synagogue**.

- The Torah scroll or **Sefer Torah** is treated with great **respect**.

- In the synagogue the Torah scroll is **read** using a **special pointer**.

Tenach

- The **Tenach** refers to the whole of the **Hebrew Bible**.

- It contains **Torah** or **Law**.

- It contains **Nevi'im** or the **Prophets**.

- Some of the great **prophets** were **Elijah**, **Nathan**, **Isaiah**, **Ezekiel** and **Jeremiah**.

- The **Tenach** contains **Ketuvim** or the **Writings**.

- Examples of the **Writings** are the **Psalms** and **Proverbs**.

Talmud

- **Talmud** means **study**.

- It contains **stories** and **teachings** of the **rabbis** on how to **keep Torah**.

- It also contains the **Oral Torah** given to **Moses** at the same time as the **Written Torah**.

6.3 Beliefs

Monotheism or the belief in one God, is the basis for all other Jewish beliefs.

God

- Jews believe that **God is one**, there are **no other gods**.

- God **created** the **world**.

- God **sees** and **knows everything**.

- **God** gave the **Torah** so **humans** are able to **worship Him** and **live life fully**.

- The **Shema** is the most **important** Jewish **prayer** which is said **daily**.

- The **Shema** remembers that God is one and **He alone** is to be **worshipped**.

Messiah

- The **Messiah** is God's **messenger of peace**.

- When he **arrives everyone** will **obey** the **commandments**.

- Jews are still **waiting** for his **arrival**.

- **Some** Jews think he will be an actual **person**.

- **Some** Jews think he is **not** an actual **person** but a **peaceful state of mind** in the world.

World to come

- The world to come is called the **Olam Ha'Ba**.

- It is a future **eternal state of the world** which will **last forever**.

- It is **not clear** exactly what this will be like.

- **Some** think it might be an **afterlife** in **heaven**.

- **Some** think it might be a **life in this world** but transformed so it is **perfect**.

6.4 Synagogue

The synagogue is more than just a place of worship. It also serves as a school and community centre.

Religious items worn by orthodox Jewish men in the synagogue

- Men wear a **hat** or **kippa** as a sign of **respect** for God.

- They wear two **special prayer boxes** or **tefillin** containing the **Shema**.

- They wear a prayer **shawl** or **tallit** with **tassels** at each corner.

Layout of a typical synagogue

- The **ark** is a **large cupboard** at the **front** of the synagogue.

- The **ark** contains the **Torah Scroll** or **Sefer Torah** and other scrolls.

- There is a **menorah** or **eight-branched candlestick**.

- The **menorah** reminds people of **God's presence**.

- In the **centre** there is a **bimah** or raised **reading platform**.

- Men and women sit **separately** in **Orthodox synagogues**.

- **Other rooms** include schoolrooms, libraries and meeting rooms.

Worship in the synagogue

- People must **dress modestly**. Boys and **men cover** their **heads**.

- Worship is set out in a **prayer book** called a **siddur**.

- In **Orthodox** synagogues the service is **led** by a **man or rabbi**.

- In **Reform** synagogues the service is **led** by any **qualified man/woman**.

- In **Orthodox** synagogues the service is mostly in **Hebrew**.

- in **Reform** synagogues the service is in a **mixture of Hebrew and English**.

- The service **begins** with the saying of several **psalms**.

- On Monday, Thursday and at Shabbat services the **Sefer Torah** is **processed** from the **ark** to the **bimah**.

- **Portions** of the **Torah** are **read** from the bimah by various people.

- The **Sefer Torah** is then **processed back to the ark**.

- On Shabbat and festival days **readings** then follow from the **prophets**.

- The **rabbi** might give a **sermon** or address.

- **Prayers** may be said for the **Royal Family**.

- The service **ends** with **Kiddush**.

- **Kiddush** is a special **blessing** made over **wine**.

6.5 Orthodox and Reform Judaism

The Reform movement started in the 19th century, and quickly spread throughout the Jewish world. Some Jewish leaders felt that certain laws needed to be revised to adapt them to the modern world. Unlike Orthodox Jews, Reform Jews do not believe that Moses was given the Torah all at once, but that many people have contributed to writing the Torah.

The beliefs of Orthodox Jews

- **God** is the **author** of the **Torah**.

- The **Torah cannot** be **changed**.

- **Moses** was also given the Oral Torah or **halakhah**.

- Men and women must **sit separately** in the synagogue.

- **Kosher laws** should be kept, e.g. milk and meat should be eaten and prepared separately.

- Women have more **laws** to fulfil at **home**.

- Men have more **laws** to fulfil in the **community**.

- Only **men** may wear **tefillin** and **tallit**.

The beliefs of Reform Jews

- The **Torah** was written **by people** at different times.

- The **Torah** can be **adapted** for modern times.

- The **Oral Torah** or **halakhah** are **human adaptations** of the Torah.

- **Kosher food laws** can be kept to but are **not always necessary**.

- **Women** may **sit with men in synagogue**.

- **Women** and **men** can become **rabbis**.

- **Women** may wear **tefillin** and **tallit**.

6.6 Family life

Family life is the most important aspect of Jewish life. There are many **commandments** (mitzvoth) which Jews follow in order for the home to be considered holy.

Mezuzah

- The **mezuzah** is a **portion** of the **Shema** written on **parchment** and is usually placed in a decorative box to keep it clean.

- The Shema is the '**hearing prayer**' found in the Torah which reminds Jews that there is only one God and that He alone should be worshipped.

- The mezuzah box should be placed on the **right-hand** side of **every door** in the home (except bathrooms).

- It **shows** that the house is a **Jewish home**.

- It is a reminder to **obey the commandments**.

Family

A father must:

- **support** his family

- study **Torah**

- make sure his **children** study Torah.

A mother must:

- **feed** the family

- make sure her husband and children wear the **right clothes**

- **prepare** the house for the **Sabbath**

- **teach daughters** what they need to know about for their future homes.

Food laws

The **Torah** lays down certain food laws:

- Kosher food means it is 'fit' or **lawful** to be eaten.

- All **blood** must be **removed from meat** before eating it.

- **Meat and milk** products must be **kept separately**.

- **Meat and milk** products must be **eaten separately** (not at the same meal).

6.7 Shabbat

The Shabbat lasts from Friday sunset until Saturday sundown. It is a day of rest and symbolises God's rest on the seventh day of Creation.

- The **mother** and **children clean and prepare** the house.

- The **Friday evening meal** and other meals are prepared.

- The **mother** lights the **Shabbat candles** and says a special **blessing** just before sunset.

- The **father** (and boys) return **from synagogue**.

- The father says **kiddush** over **wine**.

- The father then says a **blessing** over two **Hallot loaves** which are then **distributed**.

- The Shabbat **meal is eaten**.

- The **meal ends** with the singing of traditional **Jewish table songs**.

- On **Saturday** the family attends the **synagogue**.

- **Children** may attend **religion school**.

- **No work** is to be done on the Shabbat.

- The **Shabbat ends** with the ceremony of lighting a **special candle**, **smelling spices** and drinking a glass of **wine**.

6.8 Birth and Bar Mitzvah

Birth

- On the **eighth day** after birth **boys** must be **circumcised**.

- The ceremony is called **Berit Milah** and usually takes place in the **synagogue**.

- A **mohel** carries out the operation.

- A mohel is a **pious Jew** who is **skilled** at circumcisions.

- After this the child is given his **Hebrew name** and an ordinary name.

- **A blessing** is said over a cup of **wine**.

- The ceremony of circumcision represents a **covenant**, or solemn promise between God and the child, which remembers the promise made by God to **Abraham**.

Bar and Bat Mitzvah

- Bar Mitzvah (for boys) and Bat Mitzvah (for girls) are ceremonies which recognise them as adults under the Jewish Law.

- They are then responsible for their own actions and must set an example by following the commandments prescribed for them in the Torah.

- For a year before a **boy is 13** and a **girl is 12** preparation is given as to their **Jewish responsibilities**.

- On the day of the Bar Mitzvah a **boy reads publicly from the Torah** for the first time in the synagogue.

- **Girls** may read from the Torah only in **Reform synagogues**.

- **Boys** may now wear **tefillin** (prayer boxes).

- **Boys** may now wear the **tallit** (prayer shawl).

- **Relatives** attend the synagogue **service**.

- There is often a **party** afterwards.

6.9 From marriage to death

Marriage

Marriage is an important part of traditional Jewish life. Ideally the couple should both be Jewish.

- The bride and groom marry under a **canopy** or **huppah**.

- They are **led** to the **huppah** by their **families**.

- The **bride circles** the **groom**.

- A special **blessing** is made over a cup of **wine** which the **couple sip**.

- The **groom** gives a **ring** to his **bride** in front of **two witnesses**.

- The **rabbi** reads from the **ketubah** or **marriage contract**.

- The **seven blessings** are said.

- The **groom crushes glass** with his foot as a **symbol** of the destruction of the Temple in 70 CE – for some it is a reminder of what God has yet in store for the future.

- Those present shout '**mozel tov**' (congratulations).

Funeral

- **Orthodox** Jews are always **buried**.

- Some **Reform** Jews allow **cremation**.

- Burial should take place as **soon as possible**, but **not** on the **Shabbat**.

- The body is specially **prepared** and **dressed** in a **simple white garment**.

- **After** the **burial** everyone symbolically **washes** their **hands**.

- The bereaved **family** stay at **home** for a **week**.

- **Friends visit**, comfort the mourners and bring them food.

- **Men** do not **shave**.

- **Women** do not **wear make-up**.

- At the **first anniversary** (and all future anniversaries) of the death a **candle** is lit.

- The special **kaddish** prayer is said in the **synagogue** by the bereaved family.

6.10 Festivals

Festivals follow the seasons and also remember Israel's long history. They play an important part in the Jewish year and each one has its own special customs and food. There are a great number of Jewish festivals but the following are the most important:

Pesach/Passover

- Pesach is a **spring festival**.

- It remembers the time when **Moses** and the **Israelites** had to **escape** at night from **Egypt**.

- In **preparation** the house is cleaned of all **yeast** or **hametz** products.

- A special **seder** meal is **eaten** before the main meal.

- The **seder begins** when the **youngest child** asks **why this night is different** from all others.

- The story of **Exodus** is **recited** from the **haggadah** or Passover storybook.

- At various parts of the story **four cups** of **wine** are drunk to remember **God's promises**.

- Everyone eats **unleavened bread** or **matzos**.

- Everyone **dips their matzos** into herbs such as **horseradish** and **haroset**.

- Everyone eats an **egg in salt water**.

- Then the **main meal is eaten**.

- **Afterwards** everyone joins in traditional **table songs**.

Shavuot

- Shavuot is a **summer festival**.

- It takes place **50 days after Pesach**.

- It has **many purposes**.

- It remembers when **Moses** received the **Torah at Mount Sinai**.

- It is also a **harvest festival**.

- **Synagogues** and **homes** are **decorated** with **flowers**.

- It is a time to **reflect** on the **gift** of **freedom**.

- It is a time to give **thanks** for the **Torah** and to think about carrying out its **laws**.

Sukkot

- Sukkot is an **autumn festival**.

- Sukkot **remembers** the time when the Israelites **wandered in the Sinai desert**.

- The Israelites built **sukkot** or **tents** to live in.

- Today people **build sukkot** and can **live** in them for **eight days**.

- The **sukkot** are a reminder of human **dependence** on **God**.

- It is a time to **visit other** people's **sukkot**.

- In the **synagogue** people wave a bundle of **palm**, **myrtle** and **willow** branches and **carry** a **citron fruit**.

Simchat Torah

- Simchat Torah follows the festival of **Sukkot**.

- It means to **rejoice in the Law**.

- It is a time to rejoice that the weekly reading of the Torah is **complete**.

- The **Torah scroll** is **danced** round the inside of the synagogue **seven times**.

Hanukkah

- Hanukkah is a **winter festival**.

- It is a festival of **light**.

- It remembers the time when the Jews won their **freedom** from the **Greeks** in **164 BCE**.

- It remembers when **Judas Maccabee cleansed the Temple**.

- It remembers how when he lit the **menorah** with enough **oil for one day**, it burnt for **eight days**.

- Today the **Hanukkah lamp** is lit each **evening** for **eight days**.

- It is a time to **exchange presents**.

Rosh Hashanah

- Rosh Hashanah celebrates the **new year**.

- It is the beginning of a **ten-day period**.

- During this time people **apologise** and seek **forgiveness** from each other.

- It also **remembers** the **creation of the world**.

- People wear their **best clothes**.

- The festival **begins** and **ends** when a ram's horn or **shofar** is **blown**.

- The **last day** is **Yom Kippur**, the **Day of Atonement**.

- Yom Kippur is a time to **fast**, to **attend synagogue** and to **repent** of one's **sins**.

- The **Kol Nidrei** prayer is **sung** at the evening service in the synagogue.

Purim

- Purim is held in **February/March**.

- It remembers how **Queen Esther saved** the Jewish people from the **evil Haman**.

- Haman drew **lots** (or **purim**) to decide the **day** when all the **Jews** should be **killed**.

- **Esther** bravely **broke the law** and **told** her **husband** of Haman's plan.

- The main part of the synagogue **service** is **reading** the **Esther story**.

- Children **dress up** in masks and costumes to mock Haman.

- Every time **Haman's name** is mentioned people **boo and shout** to **blot out his name**. The children are allowed to bring in rattles, whistles and pan lids to do the same.

Summary

You should now know the following:

1. The place of Abraham and Moses in the origins and early history of Judaism

2. The different Jewish holy books

3. The central Jewish beliefs

4. The role of the synagogue in the Jewish community

5. The differences between Orthodox Jews and Reform Jews

6. The key beliefs and practices of Jewish family life

7. The key beliefs and practices in observing Shabbat

8. The key beliefs and practices of birth and Bar Mitzvah

9. The key beliefs and practices of marriage and death

10. The various important Jewish festivals

Test yourself

Before moving on to the next chapter, make sure you can answer the following questions. Sample answers are given on page 200.

1. Describe what happens at a Jewish funeral. (6)

2. Describe how Shabbat is celebrated at home. (6)

3. Describe what Jews believe about the Torah and the Talmud. (6)

4. Describe what Jews believe about the world to come. (6)

5. Describe any **one** important Jewish festival. (6)

Chapter 7: Islam

Chapters 4–10 cover Section 3 of the examination called 'World Religions and Contemporary Issues'. You only need to revise a minimum of **one** of these chapters for examination. If you are not sure which one to revise, then check with your teacher.

BCE means **Before the Common Era** and is equivalent to using BC.

CE means the **Common Era** and is equivalent to using AD.

In traditional Islam dates are given from the time of the migration to Makkah.

These revision notes follow the order of JF Aylett and Kevin O'Donnell's *The Muslim Experience*. You must make sure that you understand and learn the ideas in *The Muslim Experience* as well as the notes below.

7.1 God

Muslims (followers of Islam) believe the following about God:

- God's **existence cannot be proved**.

- **God** is the **creator** of everything.

- There are **no other gods**.

- **Only God** may be **worshipped and praised**.

- **God** has **99 beautiful names**.

- All the names are **found** in the **Qur'an**.

- The names describe some of God's **many characteristics**.

- The names include: The **Merciful**, The **Creator** and The **All-Knowing**.

- One of the important **metaphors for God** is **light**.

- **God** will **judge** all people according to their deeds on **earth**.

- **Prayer beads** are a **reminder** of the **99 names**.

7.2 Muhammad

Muhammad is regarded by Muslims as the last prophet of God. Muhammad's life and teaching is very important for Muslims as an example of how to live the perfect Muslim life.

Muhammad's early life

- **Muhammad** was born in **570 CE** in **Makkah**.

- His **father died before** he was **born** and his **mother died** when he was **six**.

- Eventually he was **brought up** by an uncle, **Abu Talib**.

- First he worked as a **shepherd**.

- He was very **honest** and his **uncle** let him go on **business journeys**.

- He **impressed Khadijah** and she let him **run her business**.

- He **married her** when he was **25**.

- He looked after his **uncle's son Ali**.

Muhammad's call

- **Muhammad** often went to **pray** in a **cave outside Makkah**.

- He prayed in the cave called **Hira**.

- In **610 CE** when he was **40** the **angel Gabriel** appeared to him.

- Gabriel told to him to **read** and recite.

- Muhammad **refused three times**.

- The angel squeezed **him three times**.

- Then he **recited God's words**.

- He spent some time in **shock**.

- But he was **reassured by his wife** that he had indeed **received God's word**.

Muhammad's message

- **Khadijah** and her **cousin** become the **first Muslims**.

- To begin with the **message spread slowly**.

- Muhammad **taught** the people of **Makkah not** to **worship idols**.

- This made the **merchants** of **Makkah angry**.

- The merchants considered he was **putting off pilgrims** who also **brought their business** to Makkah.

- They accused Muhammad of being **mad** and a **liar**.

- Some of his **companions** were **tortured** and **killed**.

- In **610 CE**, in the vision of the **Night Journey**, he met the great **prophets** of the **past**.

- This gave him the **confidence** to go on **preaching**.

Muhammad in Madinah and Makkah

- The people of **Yathrib** asked Muhammad to **come and settle their disputes**.

- In **622 CE** Muhammad, his family and followers went to **Yathrib**.

- The event is called the **hijrah** or migration.

- Here Muhammad started his **first Muslim community**.

- He built his first **mosque**.

- His new laws taught that under **God's rule all people** were to be treated as **equals**.

- **Yathrib** was **renamed Madinah**, or **City of the Prophet**.

- Many people were **impressed** by life at **Madinah** and **converted** to Islam.

- Muhammad **marched** on **Makkah** in **630 CE**.

- The Makkan's **gave up without** a **fight**.

- Muhammad **removed** all the **idols** from the **Ka'bah**.

- He sent out **letters** to **rulers** to become **Muslim**.

- **Muhammad died** in **632 CE**.

7.3 Qur'an and Hadith

The Qur'an

- The Qur'an is the **central holy book** of Islam.

- Qur'an means **recitation**.

- The Qur'an was **revealed** to **Muhammad** by God **through** His angel **Gabriel**.

- It was revealed gradually **over 23 years**.

- It is the **Word of God**.

- **Various people** wrote parts down.

- **Abu Bakr** ordered that a **standard copy** should be made.

- It was **checked** by those who had **heard** it **directly** from **Muhammad**.

- The copy was made less than two years after Muhammad died.

- Many **learn** the Qur'an by **heart**.

- These people are called **hafiz**.

- The Qur'an cannot be **translated** and should be **read in Arabic**.

- It is God's **final revelation** to humans.

The Qur'an used in worship

- The Qur'an is given **great respect**.

- When not in use it is kept **wrapped up**.

- It is placed on a **high shelf** to keep it **safe and clean**.

- Everyone must **wash** before reading it.

- It should be **read every day**.

- It should be **obeyed**.

The Hadith

- The **Hadith** refer to various collections of **books** of the **words and actions** of **Muhammad** himself.

- The Hadith may be consulted by Muslims to see how **Muhammad acted in various situations**.

7.4 Beliefs

Five Pillars of Faith

The Five Pillars of Faith are the five duties that apply to every Muslim. (You do not need to know the Arabic terms.)

- **Shahadah**, is the belief in **one God** and that **Muhammad is His messenger**.

- **Prayers** (salah) must be said **five times** a **day** and at the mosque.

- **Alms giving** (zakah) is a form of **tax** to **help** the poor, free people from debt etc.

- **Fasting** (sawm) must be performed during **day daylight hours** in the month of **Ramadan**.

- **Pilgrimages** (hajj) should be made to **Makkah**.

Angels

- Angels are God's **messengers**.

- They bring **God's message** to **humans** especially when they pray.

- They **cannot** usually **be seen**.

- They are made of **light** but can take on **human form**.

- They look after humans and are **felt** as **love and peace**.

God's books and prophets

- God has sent **guidance** through his **prophets**.

- Many have brought special **books** to the world.

- Great prophets include **Adam**, **Noah** and **Abraham**.

- **Moses** brought the **Law**.

- **David** brought the **Psalms**.

- **Jesus** brought the **Gospel**.

- **Muhammad** is the **last prophet**. His message **seals** the **earlier messages**.

- His message is contained in the **Qur'an**.

- Only the **Qu'ran** is a **perfect presentation** of God's word.

Last Judgement and life after death

- The Day of Judgement is when all the **dead** will be **judged**.

- Guardian **angels** keep a **record** of every person's deeds.

- Only **God** can **judge** each person's heart.

- The **good** will be rewarded with **Paradise** – a life of **peace** and **purity**.

- **Unbelievers** or the **disobedient** will be sent to **Hell** – a life of **torment**.

- Only **God** knows what is in **Paradise** and what **Hell** is really like.

The will of God

- God **created** the **world**.

- Everything is **controlled** by God at all times.

- God has **complete knowledge** of everything that happens.

- There is **no** such thing as **chance** as **God controls** the **destiny** of everything.

7.5 Salah

- Prayer or salah is the **second Pillar of Faith**.

- Prayers are said **facing** towards the **Ka'bah**.

- **Special prayers** are held on **Friday**.

- **Men** are encouraged to pray in a **mosque**.

- **Women** pray at **home**.

- Prayer can take place in **any clean place**.

- Prayer must come **from the heart**.

- **Praying together** is a sign of Muslim **unity** and **brotherhood**.

- Prayer is a **reminder** of **God's greatness** and **obedience** to Him.

- **Before** prayer a Muslim must perform **wudu** (washing of the hands, mouth, nose, face, arms, neck, behind the ears and feet).

- Prayer starts with a series of **prayer movements** called **rakat**.

- Prayers must be said **each day**:
  - between **dawn and sunrise** (Fajr)
  - after **midday** (Zuhr)
  - between late **afternoon and sunset** (Asr)
  - between **sunset and the end of daylight** (Maghrib)
  - at **night** (Isha).

7.6 Mosque

Role of the muezzin

- The **muezzin calls** people to **prayer**.

- The **call to prayer** is called the **adhan**.

- The adhan instructs the people to **rush to prayer**.

- The adhan states that '**Allah is the Greatest**; there is no God but Allah'.

- The call to prayer is usually done **from** a mosque **minaret**.

- The muezzin faces towards the **Ka'bah** in Makkah.

Layout of a typical mosque

- There is a **tower** or **minaret** for the **muezzin**.

- There are **wash rooms** and/or a fountain for special **washing** or **wudu**.

- In the **prayer hall** there is a **niche** or **mihrab** which indicates the **direction of the Ka'bah**.

- There is often a **dome** over the prayer hall.

- The **pulpit** or **minbar** in the prayer hall is for the **imam** to stand in when **preaching** and **leading the worship**.

- Mosques have **cloakrooms** for **shoes**.

- There are **separate areas** for **men** and **women**.

- There must be **no pictures**.

- The usual decorations are **abstract patterns** and elaborate **extracts** from the **Qur'an**.

7.7 Zakah

- **Zakah** (alms giving) is the **third Pillar of Faith**.

- It is a **reminder** that as everything **belongs to God**, material things are on **loan to humans**.

- It is an act of **worship** and a **duty**.

- It is a **test** to ensure that one is **not selfish**.

- Zakah is to be **paid once a year**.

- Zakah should be 2.5 per cent of one's savings.

- It is usual to give it in **secret** so one **does not get false praise**.

- The money usually goes to poor people but can also go to newly converted Muslims, or to Islamic schools, hospitals and mosques.

7.8 Sawm

- **Sawm** (fasting) is the **fourth Pillar of Faith**.

- It occurs during the month of **Ramadan**.

- Fasting is an **act of worship** and **spiritual** development.

- As it involves **suffering** it is a sign of **obedience** to God.

- Fasting helps Muslims to **appreciate the plight of the poor**.

- No food must be eaten from just **before dawn** until just **after sunset**.

- There must be no chewing of food, drinking, smoking or making love.

- Children under 12 **do not** have to **take part**.

- **Actions** as well as the fasting also matter.

- Ramadan gives a feeling of **unity** or **umma** and **common purpose** with other **Muslims**.

7.9 Hajj

- **Hajj** (pilgrimage) is the **fifth Pillar of Faith**.

- Every **adult Muslim** is expected to go on **hajj** or **pilgrimage once in a lifetime**.

- When the pilgrims arrive at **Makkah men** change into simple **white clothes**.

- This is a state of **spiritual purity** or **ihram**.

- On the **first day** pilgrims **circle** the **Ka'bah seven times**.

- Pilgrims then **run between** the **two hills** and the **Zamzam** well.

- Next they **camp out** overnight at **Muzdalifah**.

- The next day pilgrims stand in the **Plain of Arafat** and spend the day in **prayer** and **meditation**.

- On the following day they **throw stones** at the **pillars of Mina** to drive out Satan.

- On returning to **Muzdalifah** they **sacrifice** an **animal**.

- **Men** often **shave their heads**.

- Then they return to **Makkah** and **circle the Ka'bah** one last time.

- Someone who has been on a pilgrimage is called a **hajji**.

7.10 Birth and death

Birth

- When a baby is born the **father whispers** the call to prayer or **adhan** into the baby's **right ear**.

- Softened **date or honey** is **rubbed** onto the baby's **gums**.

- **Seven days** later the baby's **head is shaved**. This is called **aqiqah**.

- The baby is given a **name**.

- Names often combine **Abd**, meaning servant, with **one of God's 99 names**.

- **Boys** are then **circumcised**.

- It is a time of **celebration**.

Death

- Muslims believe in **life after death**.

- The dead person's **body** is **washed**, **anointed** and wrapped in **white sheets**.

- **Burial** takes place **as soon as possible**.

- The person is **buried** (cremation is forbidden) with their **head facing the Ka'bah**.

- As the body is **buried** the **Qur'an is recited** and earth is thrown in the grave.

- A period of **mourning** follows.

7.11 Marriage

- Marriages are **often arranged**. Love is not a primary reason for marriage.

- **Parents find** a suitable **bride/groom** for their son/daughter.

- The **husband** gives his **wife** a **dowry** (a sum of money).

- At the **wedding** people wear their **best clothes**.

- The wedding can take place at the **mosque** or at the **bride's house**.

- **Two witnesses** have to be present at the signing of the **wedding contract**.

- Passages from the **Qur'an** are **recited**.

- A **feast** is given for the relatives within three days **of the marriage**.

- **Divorce** is allowed but only as a **last resort**.

- **Men** may marry up to **four wives**, but this is **rare**.

7.12 Family life

Roles of men and women in the family

- **Both** parents must set an **example** to their **children**.

- Parents must **educate** and **feed** their **children** properly.

- **Both** parents must **respect their own parents** and be **obedient** to them.

- **Mothers** have a **responsibility** to **feed** the hungry, **look after** guests and **comfort** the distressed.

- **Husbands** must **provide money, protect** the family and be involved in the **wider world**.

- **Both** must **dress modestly**.

- There must be **no sex before marriage**.

Children's attitude to parents

- Children must **respect** their **parents**.

- Children must be **obedient** to their **parents** and **older relatives**.

- **No child** should **cause harm** to his or her parents.

- In old age **parents** may need to be **supported by their children**.

- This duty **continues** until **the parents' deaths**.

7.13 Festivals

Id-ul-Fitr

- The festival was **started** by **Muhammad**.

- It marks the **end of Ramadan**.

- It is also a time to **thank God** for the **Qur'an**.

- Muslims thank God for **getting through Ramadan**.

- Many give a special Ramadan **zakat** or gift of **money to the poor**.

- **Children** are given **presents**.

- There is **no work or school**.

- A **special midday meal** is eaten.

- It is also a special time to go to the **mosque** to **pray**.

Id-ul-Adha

- The festival takes place **towards** the **end of the hajj**.

- It is **also** celebrated by **those not on hajj**.

- **Id-ul-Adha** celebrates the time when **Abraham** was ready to **sacrifice Ishmael**.

- Abraham was willing to make this sacrifice because **God commanded** it.

- He **resisted the temptations** of the **devil** not to sacrifice Ishmael.

- This shows that **Muslims** must be **ready** to **sacrifice their lives** for God.

- The festival **begins** with **prayers** at the **mosque**.

- An **animal** is **sacrificed** to commemorate Abraham's sacrifice of an animal.

- The **meat** is **shared** with friends, relatives and the poor.

Summary

You should now know the following:

1. What Muslims believe about God

2. The role of Muhammad

3. The content of the Qur'and and Hadith

4. The central Islamic beliefs

5. The way Muslims pray

6. The role of the mosque in the Muslim community

7. The importance of zakah

8. The importance of sawm

9. What happens when a Muslim goes on hajj

10. The Muslim teaching on birth and death

11. The Muslim teaching on marriage

12. The Muslim teaching on family life

13. The main Muslim festivals

Test yourself

Before moving on to the next chapter, make sure you can answer the following questions. Sample answers are given on pages 200–201.

1. Describe what happened at Muhammad's call. (6)

2. Describe what Muslims believe about the Qur'an and Hadith. (6)

3. Explain what Muslims believe about angels. (6)

4. Describe what happens on hajj (pilgrimage). (6)

5. Describe the roles of men and women in the Muslim family. (6)

Chapter 8: Hinduism

Chapters 4–10 cover Section 3 of the examination called 'World Religions and Contemporary Issues'. You only need to revise a minimum of **one** of these chapters for examination. If you are not sure which one to revise, then check with your teacher.

> **BCE** means **Before the Common Era** and is equivalent to using BC.
>
> **CE** means the **Common Era** and is equivalent to using AD.

These revision notes follow the order of Liz Aylett and Kevin O'Donnell's *The Hindu Experience*. You must make sure that you understand and learn the ideas in *The Hindu Experience* as well as the notes below.

8.1 Holy books

The holy books of Hinduism are written in Sanskrit, an ancient language.

Vedas

- The Vedas are the **oldest** of the Hindu **holy books**.

- **Veda** means **knowledge**.

- The Vedas are believed to **come from God**.

- They provide **knowledge** of the **world**.

- They contain **hymns** and **prayers** for **priests** to sing.

- Originally they were **learnt by heart** but later they were **written down**.

- There are **four collections** of Vedas.

- The **Rig Veda** is the most **important**.

Upanishads

- The Upanishads are part of the **Vedas**, but are often considered important enough to be classed on their own.

- The **Upanishads** are written as **questions and answers** from **pupils to teachers**.

- They are **poems** written by the **holy men**.

- They **meditate** on God as **Brahman**.

- They meditate on the **meaning of life** and **reincarnation**.

Smirtis

- The **smirtis** were written by **holy men** as **commentaries** to explain the **Vedas**.

- They were written **2500 years** ago.

- They are **not** always **easy** to **understand**.

- Simpler books were written containing stories.

- The **Ramayana** is a collection of **stories** and **poems** about the **ancient heroes**.

- Another **important story** is the **Mahabharata**.

The Mahabharata

- The **Mahabharata** is smirti. It is one of the longest poems ever produced.

- The story tells the **history** of ancient **India**.

- The eldest **Kuru** brother, **Dhritavashtra**, was **blind** so could **not rule effectively**.

- Instead his **brother Pandu became king**.

- But Pandu wanted to be a **holy man**.

- So he **gave** his **kingdom** back to his **brother**.

- Dhritavashtra looked after **Pandu's five sons**.

- His **own sons** became very **jealous** and wanted to **kill Pandu's sons**.

- Pandu's sons escaped to the **forest led by Prince Arjuna**.

- The **blind king gave Pandu's sons half his kingdom** but the **Kurus stole it**.

- A **great battle** followed between the **Kurus** and **Pandavas** (the **sons of Pandu**).

- The **Pandavas won** and **ruled wisely**.

- The story is about the **battle** between **good and evil**.

Bhagavad Gita

- One **chapter** of the **Mahabharata** is the **Bhagavad Gita**.

- Bhagavad Gita means **Song of the Lord**.

- It is a **poem** in which **Arjuna** is about to **enter** a **battle** but does not want to kill his own relations.

- **Arjuna** therefore turns to **Krishna** for **advice**.

- **Krishna** is in the form of his **chariot driver** and **teaches** him.

- **Krishna** then **reveals himself as God**.

- He tells **Arjuna** that he must **fulfil** his **duty** as a prince and **fight**.

- He explains that **no one can kill** the **soul**.

- He explains that **life** is only **worthwhile** in **loving and worshipping God**.

- **Arjuna** goes on to **fight** and **win**.

8.2 Beliefs

Brahman

- Hindus believe in **one God** who manifests himself in **many forms**.

- The **forms** are the **deities** such as **Vishnu, Shiva, Durga** and **Krishna**.

- **Brahman** is the **invisible** aspect of God.

- **Aum** represents the **mystical vibration** of God/Spirit in the universe.

- **Brahman** is this **spirit or life force**.

- **Brahman** is the **origin of everything**.

- **Brahman** is in **everything** but **cannot be seen**.

- **Brahman** is both **personal** or **impersonal**.

- The **worship of Brahman** is called **bhakti**.

Atman and samsara

- **Every** living **thing** has **atman**.

- **Atman** is **soul** and is **part of Brahman**.

- This means we **all** have an **aspect of God within** us.

- When the body of a living thing **dies**, its **atman moves on** to **another body**.

- This is called **samsara** or **reincarnation**.

- **Samsara** also describes the **changes we go through in life** as our bodies change.

- Our **characters** may change but deep down we are the **same person** or **atman**.

Karma

- **Karma** is the **law of cause and effect**.

- Karma affects **samsara** and how we behave in a **reincarnated life**.

- A **good life** now means the **next life** will be **happier or better**.

- A **bad life** now means the **next life** will be **unhappier or unlucky**.

- **Bad karma** could even result in being reincarnated as a **lower life form**.

Dharma

- **Dharma** means **duty** and doing what is **morally right**.

- **Dharma** is informed by **conscience** and the **scriptures**.

- **Dharma** also describes Hinduism as **Eternal Truth**.

Ahimsa

- **Ahimsa** means **non-violence**.

- As all living things have **atman** so they must all be **treated with respect**.

- Sometimes this causes **moral problems**.

- **Arjuna** had to decide between his **duty not to harm** and his **duty to fight against evil**.

Environment

- Hindus believe we should all be **grateful** for **God's gifts in nature**.

- All **living things** have a soul or **atman**.

- So **humans** have a responsibility to **look after nature**.

- Humans must only accept those things **given to them**.

- **Earth** is 'our mother' and **humans are 'her children'**.

- **Offerings** should be given to **sacred areas in nature**.

- **Killing living things** can result in **bad karma**.

Cows and vegetarianism

- **Cows** are **sacred** because they provide for **human needs**.

- They provide **milk**.

- They provide **butter**.

- They provide **ghee**, which is used for **offerings to the deities**.

- They pull **carts**.

- They are seen as **mothers**.

- They are a **gift from God**.

- **Respect** for the **cow** and other **living beings** means Hindus should be **vegetarians**.

8.3 Caste and dharma

- There are **four castes** or **varnas**.

- Each caste is associated with **specific jobs** or roles.
    - **Brahmins** are **priests** and **teachers**.
    - **Kshatriyas** are **rulers** and **fighters**.
    - **Vaishyas** are **farmers** and **traders**.
    - **Shudras** are **workers**.
    - **Untouchables** are **casteless** and not members of the varnas.

- Each caste has specific **duties** or **dharma** it has to carry out.

- Carrying out one's caste duties affects one's **karma** and therefore one's **caste in the next life**.

- It is **illegal in India today** to **discriminate** against someone because of their **caste**.

- Some teach a **more spiritual version** of the varnas which says you can **change caste** by developing different **attitudes** and **skills**.

8.4 Goal

- Hindus believe that every living thing has a **goal** to reach during a lifetime – this is called **Moksha**.

- **Moksha** means **release** from **samsara** – the **cycle of rebirths**.

- When the soul or **atman** is **pure** it is **released** to become **one with God**.

- There are **three paths** to moksha:
    - the way of **action**, good works or **karma**
    - the way of **knowledge** or **jnana**
    - the way of **devotion** or **bhakti**.

- **Moksha** is also achieved through **meditation** and **bodily control** or **raja**.

8.5 God

- Hindus believe in only **one God.**

- God has **many aspects**, however, so he can appear and be worshipped in **many forms**.

- Some believe all gods are **forms** of **Brahman**.

- Each Hindu is a **devotee** to a **particular form**.

- The most **popular** deities are **Vishnu** and **Shiva**.

Brahman

- **Brahman** is symbolised by **fire** and the sound **aum**.

Vishnu

- Some worship **Vishnu** as the supreme form of God.

- He is **preserver** of the cosmos.

- He is an aspect of **Supreme Being** or **Brahman**.

- His **four arms** symbolise **power**.

- His **conch** shell symbolises **worship**.

- He comes to Earth in **ten** various **forms** or **avatars**.

- **Six avatars** are **animal** or semi-human, **four** are **human**.

- Avatars include the **dwarf**, **Rama** and **Krishna**.

- **Lesser deities** are called **mahatmas** or **great souls**.

Shiva

- Some worship **Shiva** as the supreme form of God.

- He is shown as a **dancing figure**.

- His **dance** symbolises the **power of creation**.

- He holds a **drum** which symbolises the **rhythm of life**.

- The **ring of fire** which surrounds him symbolises his **power to create and destroy**.

Paths to God

- The paths to God represent the three ways in which a person can achieve moksha.

- The **three paths** are: **karma, jnana** and **bhakti**.

- That means as God is **active** we must offer our hard **work** to God.

- That means as God is **knowledge** we must offer our **minds** to God.

- That means as God is **love** we must offer our **worship** to God.

8.6 From birth to death

- Hindus divide a lifetime up into stages, each of which corresponds with an **important life event**.

- Each **stage of life** is called a **samskara**.

- There are **16 samskaras**.

Birth

- When a **baby is born** the **priest** works out a **horoscope** to see how the planets will affect the person's life.

- The horoscope tells the parents which **letter** their **child's name** should begin with.

- Some **choose names** after the **gods or deities** such as Lakshmi or Krishna.

Initiation or the sacred thread ceremony

- This takes place for a **boy** sometime between his **eighth and eleventh birthday**.

- This is the **10th samskara**.

- The ceremony is only for those boys who belong to the **first three castes** or varnas.

- The **thread** consists of **three strands** (white, red and yellow) which are reminders of the boy's **three duties**:

  - **his first** duty to **God**

  - **his second** duty to his **parents**

  - **his third** duty to his religious **teachers**.

- The **ceremony** is held at **home**.

- The **thread** is placed over the boy's **left shoulder** by his **priest or teacher**.

- The boy will **wear the thread all his life**.

- It is a **sign** that he is now an **adult**.

Marriage

- It is a **duty** of Hindu **men to marry**.

- Marriages are often **arranged**.

- **Love develops** later in a relationship.

- The bride's wedding preparations involve:
  - bathing **in perfumed water**
  - rubbing her skin with **tumeric powder**
  - wearing her **best sari**
  - painting **patterns** on her hands with **henna**.

- Weddings often take place at night.
  - At the ceremony the couple take **seven steps** round a **fire** which represents **God's presence**.
  - This symbolises their hope for **children, wealth, happiness** etc.
  - As they do this they **carry a scarf** to symbolise how their lives are **joined together**.
  - The **final step** marks the moment when they become **husband and wife**.
  - **Rice grain** is sprinkled over the couple as a sign of **fertility**.
  - Afterwards some couples put their **handprints on the bride's parents'** house as a **sign** that she has **left home**.

Death

- Some men choose to **stay as householders**, but when the children have left home they devote more time to God and go on **pilgrimage**.

- Some **give** up **all home life** and become **sanyasi**. This is the **14th samskara**.

- When a person **dies** their body is **washed** and dressed in **fresh clothes**.

- **Flowers** are put round the body.

- The **16th samskara** is cremation when the body is put on a **funeral pyre**.

- The **ashes** should be **scattered** in **a holy river**.

- Cremation **releases the soul** for the next stage of its journey.

8.7 Pilgrimage

- Pilgrimage is the act of making a journey to a place which has special religious significance.

- People who make these journeys are known as **pilgrims**.

- Most pilgrimages **end** with a visit to a **temple**.

- There are **many temples** but the important ones are **Badrinath, Rameshwaram**, **Puri** and **Dwarka**.

- Pilgrimage is a sign of **religious dedication** as it costs time and money.

- Pilgrimage is **social** but **also** a time of **spiritual cleansing**.

- Some pilgrims visit **special places** like the river **Ganges** and the holy city of **Varanasi**.

- Some pilgrims visit **Jagannath** where there is a huge **image** of **Krishna**.

8.8 Festivals

New year

- New year is usually celebrated in **March/April**.

- Many **families** make a **banner** and hang it above the door.

- Some make **Rangoli** or special **patterns** outside their houses to welcome the new year.

Dassehra

- Dassehra is celebrated towards the end of **October**.

- It commemorates the story of **Rama**.

- Many **act out** the story.

- Some make **models** of the evil **Ravana** which they smash.

- Some **burn** large pictures of **Ravana** filled with **fireworks**.

Divali

- Divali takes place in late **autumn**.

- It lasts **between two and five days**.

- People light **oil lamps** or **Divas**.

- The **lamps** are placed on **window ledges or by doors**.

- The **light** commemorates how **Rama** was **welcomed home** after he **defeated Ravana**.

- The **lights** are also to welcome **Lakshmi** to people's homes.

- The Divali is the **story recited** to remember how evil was destroyed by good.

- Many set off **fireworks**.

Holi

- Holi is a **spring festival**.

- It is named after the evil **Princess Holika**.

- She tried to **kill her nephew** but was burned in a fire.

- Large **bonfires** are lit on the **eve** of the festival.

- **Krishna's** life is **remembered**.

- **The morning after** is a time for **practical jokes**.

- **Children** are allowed to be **cheeky to adults**.

8.9 Worship at home

- **Worship** is called **puja**.

- Most Hindus perform worship at home once or twice a day.

- **Families** are usually **devoted** to **one** particular **deity**.

- Many have a **shrine** at home.

- The **shrine** contains images of the **family's** favourite **deity** or **deities**.

- **Each day** the deity is **woken up** and a **lamp** is **lit**.

- The image or **murti** is **washed** and **dressed**.

- **Flowers** are offered and **incense** burned.

- Special **food** is **offered** and **blessed**.

- **Prashad** (blessed food) is **eaten** by the **family**.

- **Prayers** may be in the form of a **mantra** or chant.

- Some practise **yoga** or **meditation** instead.

- At the **end of the day puja** is performed and the image is **put away** for the **night**.

8.10 Temple

Typical Hindu temple

- A temple is **dedicated** to a particular **god or goddess**.

- It is the **home** of the deity's **image** or **murti**.

- The temple is sometimes called a **mandir**.

- A **priest's** role is to **look after** the **murti**.

- Every day he **prepares** the **murti** ready **for worshippers**.

- The **temple** is **built** to symbolise the meeting of **heaven and earth**.

- The temple **spires** also symbolise the **journey of the soul to moksha**.

- It contains **carvings** from the **animal, human** and **divine worlds**.

- It is usually very **tall** like a **mountain range**.

- The **porch** contains the 'vehicle' or **vihara** of the deity.

- The **main hall** or **mandapa** often has **pillars**.

- The **inner shrine**, the '**womb**' or **shikara**, contains the **image** of the deity.

Worship in the temple

- **Worship** in the temple is very similar to **puja at home**.

- People take their **shoes off** before entering the **mandapa**.

- Each person **rings a bell** to **tell** the **deity** that they have **arrived**.

- Some **pray** by **themselves** or in **family groups**.

- Some people **meditate quietly**, others **sing hymns or prayers**.

- **Hindu scriptures** are read at various times.

- The **priest** performs **arti** by passing round a lamp and people place their hands near it.

- The **light** and **fire** symbolise the **presence of the deity**.

- The **priest** makes **daily offerings** of **incense, fire** and **water**.

- The **worshippers offer gifts** of **money, food** and **flowers**.

- The **priest** offers worshippers **prashad** (blessed food) in return.

- The **priest** prepares the **deity** for the **night**.

Summary

You should now know the following:

1. The different Hindu holy books

2. The key Hindu beliefs

3. The importance and relationship of caste and dharma

4. The significance of moksha

5. The idea of God in Hinduism

6. Hindu ceremonies from birth to death

7. The key events of pilgrimages

8. The various Hindu festivals

9. Puja or Hindu worship at home

10. The role of the temple in Hindu life

Test yourself

Before moving on to the next chapter, make sure you can answer the following questions. Sample answers are given on pages 201–202.

1. Describe the story in the Mahabharata (6)

2. Explain the Hindu teaching on atman and samsara (reincarnation). (6)

3. Describe **one** Hindu festival. (6)

4. Describe what happens at a typical Hindu wedding. (6)

5. Describe worship in a Hindu temple. (6)

Chapter 9: Buddhism

Chapters 4–10 cover Section 3 of the examination called 'World Religions and Contemporary Issues'. You only need to revise a minimum of **one** of these chapters for examination. If you are not sure which one to revise, then check with your teacher.

> **BCE** means **Before the Common Era** and is equivalent to using BC.
>
> **CE** means the **Common Era** and is equivalent to using AD.

These revision notes follow the order of Mel Thompson's *The Buddhist Experience*. You must make sure that you understand and learn the ideas in *The Buddhist Experience* as well as the notes below.

9.1 Siddhartha

- Siddhartha, who became the **Buddha**, is the central figure of Buddhism.

- His example is sometimes used as a **parable** to show how people can live their lives and aim for enlightenment.

- **Siddhartha's father** was **ruler** of the **Northern Indian** clan.

- He was **brought up** in **luxury**.

- A **wise man** said Siddhartha would grow up to be a **religious teacher** and would give **away all his possessions** and **power**.

- He **trained** in the **martial arts**.

- He **married** at a young age and had a **child**.

- His **father stopped** him seeing what lay **outside** the **palace**.

- He gave him every **luxury** so **Siddhartha would not** be **interested** in **religion**.

Siddhartha's quest

- **Siddhartha** was not happy and **wanted** to **see outside** the palace.

- He set out from his palace and saw **four sights**:
    - an **old person**
    - a **sick person**
    - a **dead person**
    - a **holy man**.

- **Siddhartha** set out as a **homeless wanderer** at the age of **29**.

- He lived an **ascetic** life, avoiding physical pleasures, **eating almost nothing** and focusing on **prayer**.

- But **after six years** he realised that this did **not bring enlightenment**.

The Enlightened One

- **Siddhartha** was **abandoned** by his **five companions**.

- He **sat** at the **foot** of a **Bo-Tree**.

- He **vowed** he would **stay there** until he had **discovered** the **truth**.

- He experienced many **temptations** throughout the **night**.

- He saw **visions** of things of the **past**, his many **previous lives** and **suffering**.

- At **dawn** he believed he had achieved **enlightenment**.
    - He realised that the **cause of suffering** is **craving**.
    - He realised that **everything affects everything** else.
    - He realised that everything **changes**, including ourselves.

- He was now called the **Buddha** or **Enlightened One**.

9.2 Dharma

- Dharma is the term used for the **Buddha's teaching**.

- It means the **Path of Awakening**.

- By following dharma, Buddhists hope to achieve **enlightenment**.

Three Universal Truths

- The **First Universal Truth is anicca:** everything **changes**.
    - Everything changes because everything is **dependent** on everything else.

- The **Second Universal Truth is anatta:** there is **no enduring self or soul**.
    - We have **no souls** because people change and things change.

- The **Third Universal Truth is dukkha:** there is **suffering**.
    - There is suffering because everything changes and things **die**.

Four Noble Truths

- The **First Noble Truth is that** all life involves **suffering** or **dukkha**.

- The **Second Noble Truth is that** the origin of suffering is **craving** or **tanha**.

- The **Third Noble Truth is that** if **craving goes** so does suffering.

- The **Fourth Noble Truth is that** the **Middle Way** or Eightfold Path is the middle way between extremes.
  - The **extremes** are **luxury** and **hardship**.
  - **Extremes do not bring enlightenment**, only the middle way does.

The Noble Eightfold Path

- The Noble Eightfold Path is the middle path **between extremes**.
- It is the **fourth** element of the **Four Noble Truths**.
- The path gives advice for **everyday living**.
- The path also helps **train the mind** with the right:
  - **view**
  - **intention**
  - **speech**
  - **action**
  - **livelihood**
  - **effort**
  - **mindfulness**
  - **contemplation**.

Karma

- **Karma** is the **law** of **cause and effect**.
- Actions have **consequences** for **oneself** and **others now** and in **future** lives.
- The **Noble Eightfold Path** gives **guidance** to be aware of **karma**.

The Triple Way

- Way 1: **Morality** – how to treat **others**
- Way 2: **Meditation** – how to **think** clearly
- Way 3: **Wisdom** – how to **reflect** on one's life

Nirvana

- **Rebirth** occurs when a person lives a **life** of **greed** and **ignorance** ('the fires').
- **Nirvana** is a state when greed and **ignorance** are no longer experienced.
- **Nirvana** means '**blowing out**'.
- **Nirvana** is a state of **contentment**.
- **Nirvana** can only be **achieved** when a person is **enlightened**.

9.3 Sangha

- **Sangha** means **community**.
- The **first followers** of **Buddha** were called the **sangha**.
- All **members** are **equal**.
- **Sangha** gives **support** to all to achieve **enlightenment**.
- **Some** choose to become **monks** or **bhikkhus**.
- **Some** choose to become **nuns** or **bhikkhunis**.
- **Monks study** the **dharma** in Buddhist **monasteries** or **viharas**.
- **Monks** and **nuns** have a special **responsibility** to **teach dharma**.
- **Sangha also refers** to the worldwide community of **all Buddhists**.

9.4 Types of Buddhism

- Most traditions **distinguish** between Buddhist **monks/nuns** and ordinary or **lay** Buddhists.
- The **three main traditions** are: **Theravada**, **Mahayana** (Pure Land and Zen) and **Tibetan**.
- **Western** Buddhism is a mixture of all three traditions.

Theravada Buddhism

- Theravadan Buddhism is the oldest form of Buddhism that is still followed today.
- It places **importance** on the practice of **meditation**.
- It considers that being a **monk** is an **ideal** way of being a Buddhist.
- **Monks** wear **saffron robes**.
- They **shave** their **heads**.
- They live in **monasteries**.
- They receive **food** from **lay people**.
- They use **beads** for **meditation**.
- Many become **lay monks** for a while to **learn dharma** and then **leave** the monastery.

Mahayana Buddhism

- Mahayanan Buddhism was probably formed in Southern India in the 1st century CE.

- It is aimed at **lay people** not just monks or nuns.

- **Pure Land Buddhism** believes in devotion to **Amida Buddha**.

- Pure Land Buddhists:

  - chant '**Nembutsu**' as a form of **meditation**.

  - believe this will **help** them **enter 'Buddha Land'** – a state free from troubles.

- **Zen Buddhism** is popular in **Japan**.

- Zen teaches:

  - that **everyone** has a **Buddha nature**.

  - that it is through **training** the **mind** that a person can **discover** their Buddha nature.

  - us to be **aware of every action**.

  - that **awareness** can be **achieved** through **simple actions** such as **making tea** and **arranging flowers**.

Tibetan Buddhism

- Tibetan Buddhism is similar to Mahayanan Buddhism in that it is not just aimed at monks and nuns.

- **Tibetan** Buddhism stresses the **importance** of **images** and wall-hangings for **meditation**.

- It uses **chants** or **mantras** in worship.

- There is often a lot of **dancing**, **music** and **processions** at **festivals**.

- Tibetan Buddhists use **prayer wheels**.

- The **monks** are very keen on **debates** in monasteries.

- **Senior teachers** are called **lamas**.

- The most **famous lama** is the **Dalai Lama**.

Western Buddhism

- Buddhism spread to the West mostly through Indian and Chinese immigrants during the 20th century.

- **All types** of Buddhism are practised in the West.

- **Friends of the Western Buddhist Order** (FWBO) **mix** all three **traditions**.

- The FWBO **adapts** the three traditions for use in the West.

- When people first join they are called '**Friends**'.

- The FWBO do **not have monks or nuns**.

- **Some** live in **single sex communities**.

- **Many** continue to live in their **own families**.

9.5 Refuge

- When a person **chooses** the **Buddhist way of life** they make a solemn **declaration** called 'taking refuge'.

- This means **facing life** and putting the **Buddha's teaching** into **practice**.

- In front of an **ordained Buddhist** they say:
    - 'I **go to the Buddha**'
    - 'I **go to the dharma**'
    - 'I **go to the sangha**'.

- **Offerings** are made of **candles**, **flowers** and **incense**.

- A Buddhist **promises** to live a life of **compassion** for other **humans**.

- A Buddhist **promises** to help and **respect all creatures**.

9.6 Buddha images

Use of images

- The Buddha is never worshipped in Buddhism but various images are very helpful for **education** and **mediation**.

- **Some** images are:
    - of the **historical Buddha**
    - **symbols** of the **inner experiences** of the Buddha
    - **expressions** of **bodhisattvas,** that is all those who have become **enlightened**.

- **Some** Buddhists like to **meditate** using **several images**.

- **Some** meditate just using an image of the **historical Buddha**.

Types of images

- The **angry Buddha** helps to direct **anger** in a **positive way**.

- **Bodhisattva Manjogosha** shows how the **sword of wisdom cuts** through **ignorance**.

- The **Yab-Yum** picture of a sexual couple shows a **relationship** of **wisdom** and **compassion**.

Symbols

- The **flame** from Buddha's head is a symbol of **enlightenment**.

- An image with a **thousand arms** symbolises the **help** given by a **bodhisattva** in any situation.

- An image of **stepping down** is a symbol of the way a **bodhisattva** comes to **help** people.

- A **vajra** or **thunderbolt** is a sign of **determination**.

- A **lotus flower** is a sign of **enlightenment** and of the journey of the mind from **ignorance** to **wisdom**.

- The **eight-spoked wheel** represents the **eightfold path**.

9.7 Shrines, temples and monuments

For some Buddhists the temple is the centre of worship outside of the home. The temple contains a shrine room, in which Buddhist imagery is found. A home may also have a shrine to the Buddha.

Worship or puja

- **Temples** have **rooms** for **chanting** and **meditating**.

- In a **temple** there is often much chanting of **mantras**.

- A common mantra is: **Om mani padme hum**.

- **Offerings** are made to the **image of a Buddha**.

- Devotees **listen** to the Buddhist **scriptures**.

Shrines

- A shrine might include:
  - **Buddha images**
  - **seven offering bowls** set in **front** of the **Buddha image**
  - **flowers**, **candles** and **incense** which are traditional **offerings**
  - **cushions** for **meditation**
  - a **bell** to tell when the **next stage** of **puja** is to start.

- In a **shrine room** people turn to the shrine and put their **hands together** as a sign of **respect**.

Monuments

- **Monuments** or **stupas** contain a **relic** of the **Buddha**, such as a part of his clothing etc.

- **Pilgrims** walk **round the outside** of monuments.

9.8 Festivals

- There are **no fixed rules** for Buddhist festivals.

- Festival **ceremonies** are **not essential**.

- What matters is a **state of mind** and **celebrating together**.

Festival of Wesak

- Wesak is celebrated at the **full moon** in **May**.

- It remembers the **birth of the Buddha**.

- It celebrates the **Buddha's enlightenment** and **death**.

- There are **joyful processions**.

- People **decorate** their **local shrines** and **homes**.

Festival of New Year

- The new year is mostly celebrated in **Thailand** in **April**.

- **Water** is used to wash **Buddha images**.

- People **splash each other**.

- **Stranded fish** are **put back** into **rivers**.

- **Water** is used because it is a **symbol** of **new life** and **refreshment**.

Festival of the Full Moon

- This festival celebrates the **beginning** of the **Buddha's teaching** or **dharma**.

Festival of Kathina

- For this festival **monks** and **nuns** go on **retreat**.

- People make **offerings** of **practical things** to the **monasteries**.

9.9 Buddhist way of life

The Five Precepts or skills

The Five Precepts govern how a Buddhist ought to live if he or she is to achieve a balanced life and perhaps even enlightenment.

- Avoid **taking life**.

- Avoid **taking what is not given**.

- Avoid **harmful sexual activity**.

- Avoid **telling lies**.

- Avoid **alcohol** and **drugs**.

Right Livelihood

- Buddhists must choose a career carefully if they are to follow the **Five Precepts**.

- Jobs to be avoided might include: army, working in a pub, working as a butcher.

- They should also **apply** the **Five Precepts** in **business**.

Environment

- Buddhism teaches that everything is **dependent on everything else**, so humans are not superior to anything else.

- The **world** is therefore **not just** there **for humans**.

- This is why **humans** have a **duty to care** for the **environment**.

- Buddhists should show **loving kindness** to all **creatures**.

- Buddhists should try **not** to **damage the Earth**.

- The aim should be to enable all things to **live** in **harmony**.

- Some Buddhists choose to be **vegetarians** out of **respect for life**.

9.10 Scriptures

- The **earliest scriptures** are called **Tripitaka** or **Three Baskets**.
  - The **first basket** has **rules** for **monks** and **nuns**.
  - The **second basket** has the **teachings** of the **Buddha**.
  - The second basket also contains the **Dhammapada** and is the most **popular Buddhist scripture**.

- The second basket also contains the **Jataka Tales.** These are **stories** of the **former lives** of the **Buddha**.

- The **third basket** is Buddhist **philosophical teaching**.

- **Zen Buddhists do not have scriptures** but rely on the teachings of **teachers** that have been **handed down**.

- **Japanese** Buddhists use **koans** which are **short questions** or **sayings**.

- One **famous** koan is, '**What is the sound of one hand clapping?**'.

Summary

You should now know the following:

1. The life and role of Siddhartha (the Buddha) in Buddhism

2. The main teachings of the dharma

3. The importance of the sangha

4. The various types of Buddhism

5. The meaning of 'taking refuge'

6. The various types of Buddha images and their meanings

7. The use of the shrine or temple in Buddhist life

8. The main Buddhist festivals

9. How Buddhists live their lives

10. The different Buddhist scriptures

Test yourself

Before moving on to the next chapter, make sure you can answer the following questions. Sample answers are given on page 202.

1. Describe Siddhartha's (the Buddha's) quest and the four sights. (6)

2. Explain what is meant by the sangha. (6)

3. Describe briefly any **two** different kinds of Buddhism. (6)

4. Explain Buddhists' use of images in worship. (6)

5. Describe the main teachings on the Buddhist way of life. (6)

Chapter 10: Sikhism

Chapters 4–10 cover Section 3 of the examination called 'World Religions and Contemporary Issues'. You only need to revise a minimum of **one** of these chapters for examination. If you are not sure which one to revise, then check with your teacher.

BCE means **Before the Common Era** and is equivalent to using BC.

CE means the **Common Era** and is equivalent to using AD.

These revision notes follow the order of Philip Emmett's *The Sikh Experience*. You must make sure that you understand and learn the ideas in *The Sikh Experience* as well as the notes below.

10.1 Guru Nanak

- **Guru Nanak** was born near **Lahore** in **1469 CE** in **Pakistan**.

- He was the first of the **ten gurus (religious teachers)**.

- He was the **son** of **high caste Hindu** parents.

- His **intelligence** and **wisdom impressed his teachers** at an early age.

- One story tells how, as a **child**, a **deadly cobra shaded** him from the **sun**.

- On one occasion he used his pocket **money to help the poor**.

- He **married** when he was **16**.

- He became an **accountant** for a **Muslim leader**.

- He was well **known** for his **honesty**.

- He **prayed** a lot and one day, when he came out a **river**, he felt the strong **presence of God**.

- **Three days later** he set out to **teach** people how to **pray, live pure lives** and **give generously**.

- He went on **four great teaching journeys** accompanied by his **friend** and musician **Mardana**.

- In **1521 CE** he **founded** a new town, **Kartarpur**, as the **first Sikh community**.

- The first **free kitchen** or **langar** was founded. Free meals were served to visitors.

- He **died** in **1539 CE**.

- He appointed **Lehna** to be his **successor**.

10.2 Guru Angad

- **Angad** was **appointed** to be guru just **before Guru Nanak died.**

- He was called **Lehna** but was **renamed Angad** which means '**part of my body**'.

- He was a man of **humility**, **devotion** and **commitment.**

- He **taught** people that **salvation** is achieved through **performing their duties.**

- He taught his **disciples** to be **physically fit.**

- He **collected** together **Guru Nanak's hymns.**

- These hymns are **collected** in the **Guru Granth Sahib.**

- He **developed** the **free kitchen.**

10.3 Guru Gobind Rai

- Guru Gobind Rai was the **last** of the **ten gurus.**

- He was **later called Guru Gobind Singh.**

- He was a **strong leader** and **challenged** the **emperor.**

- He restored the Sikh's faith in God.

- He **trained Sikhs** to be **soldiers** to protect the rights and beliefs of others.

- He wrote **poetry** to give **spiritual strength.**

- The **Sikhs** grew in **confidence** under his leadership.

Vaisakhi 1699 CE

- A large number of **Sikhs** had **met** to **celebrate Vaisakhi** (the Sikh new year) in **1699 CE.**

- **Gobind Rai** asked for **volunteers** who would **give** their **heads** for him.

- **Five volunteers** presented themselves and each time **Gobind Rai appeared** with a **sword dripping** with the **blood** of the volunteer.

- Then the **five men** appeared **unharmed.**

- These five men were the **formation** of the **Panj Pyares** or 'five beloved ones'.

- They became the **basis** of the **Khalsa** or '**pure community**'.

- The five become **members** of the **Khalsa** by eating a **special food** called **Amrit.**

- All members of the **Khalsa** are called **Singh** (lion) or **Kaur** (princess).

- Gobind Rai insisted on **high standards of dress**.

- **Gobind Rai** was **murdered** in **1708 CE** by one of his enemies.

- He said in the **future** there would be **no more gurus**.

- He said the guru would be the **Sikh scriptures**, or the **Guru Granth Sahib**.

10.4 The Khalsa

- The **Khalsa** is a body of dedicated Sikhs who are **willing to die for** the **Guru** and **Sikhism**.

- **Not all Sikhs** are members of the **Khalsa**.

- **Khalsa** members adopt the **new name** of **Singh** or **Kaur**.

- They have to **live** to **high moral standards**.

- **Singh** means **lion** and describes how **men** are to be strong, caring and fearless.

- **Kaur** means **princess** and describes how **women** should be treated like a princess.

- Male and female members of the Khalsa **wear five symbols**, the five Ks.

The five Ks

- **Kesh** – **uncut hair** – a sign of saintliness as it is a gift from God.

- **Kangha** – **comb** – keeps uncut hair tidy. Men wear turbans.

- **Kara** – **steel band** on the right hand – a sign that **God is eternal** and a sign of the **unity** and strength of the Khalsa.

- **Kachha** – **shorts** (underclothes) – a sign of **duty** to others and action.

- **Kirpan** – **sword** – a sign of **freedom** and a duty to **protect the weak**.

10.5 Guru Granth Sahib

- **Guru** means **religious teacher**.

- The role of the guru is to **lead** people from **darkness into light**.

- There were **no more human gurus after the death of the tenth Guru Gobind Singh**.

- The role of the guru was **carried on** by the **Sikh scriptures** – the **Guru Granth Sahib**.

- The **scriptures** include the **teachings** of the **first five gurus**.

- These teachings were **first compiled** by **Guru Arjan**.

- The Guru Granth Sahib contains many **hymns** arranged according to their **tunes** or **ragas**.

- It is written in the **Gurmukhi script**.

- It is **respected** but **not worshipped**.

- It is considered to be the **word of God**.

- It is given the **place of honour** in the **gurdwara**.

- It must be **present** at all **important ceremonies**.

- When **moved** at a ceremony, it **must be carried on a person's head**.

- It must be **wrapped in clean decorated cloths**.

- Its teachings are called **gurbani**.

- Many Sikhs have a separate room at **home** called a **gurdwara** in which they read the **Guru Granth Sahib**.

- Many **homes** keep and read a **shortened version** called the **Gutka**.

10.6 Rahit Maryada

- **Rahit** means **discipline**.

- The Rahit Maryada is a **code of conduct** for Sikhs.

- In the **first Khalsa** Guru Gobind Singh laid down clear rules.

- Over time some **new rules** were added which caused **dispute**.

- In **1945 the rules** were **made clear** in the **Rahit Maryada**.

- It has been **translated** into **English**.

- It explains that a **Sikh** is anyone who believes in **one God**, the **ten gurus'** teaching, the **Guru Granth Sahib** and **baptism** by **Amrit** and is **not a member of another religion**.

- It expects **Sikhs** to **meet together** and **think** about **gurbani**, the teaching of the Guru Granth Sahib.

The Rahit's teaching on Sikh family life

- A Sikh must **pray to God** before carrying out any task.

- **Children** must be **educated**.

- **Children's hair** should **not be cut**.

- **No Sikh** should take any **drug, alcohol or tobacco**.

- **Women** may **not pierce their bodies** for jewellery.

- **Women** may **not wear** a **face veil**.

The Rahit's teaching on life in the community

- Every Sikh must give **money to help the poor**.

- There must be **no gambling**.

- Sikhs should **never steal**.

- Every Sikh should aim to be involved with **voluntary work**.

10.7 Beliefs

God

- Beliefs about God are found in the **Mul Mantra prayer** written by **Guru Nanak**.

  - God is **Truth**.

  - There is **only one** God.

  - God is the **beginning and end** of everything.

  - God is the **designer** and **creator**.

  - God is **timeless**.

  - God is **self-existent** (He does not depend on anything else for His existence).

  - God's **name** is most important and should be remembered and **repeated** by Sikhs.

  - God's name is remembered by reciting the **Waheguru** or **Wonderful Lord**.

Reincarnation

- **Reincarnation** is **rebirth** and refers to those who have been **selfish and ignored God's will**.

- Rebirth is caused by being **envious** of others or by greed.

- **Mukti** means **release from rebirth**.

- **Mukti** is **given by God's grace**.

- **Release** comes by **listening** to the **gurbani**.

- Release also comes by listening and **meditating** on the **name of God**.

Gurus

- A **guru** is a **religious leader**.

- It is important for a Sikh to have a good **upright person** as their guru.

- The guru **leads** people from **dark to light**.

- The guru **teaches** people about the **Guru Granth Sahib**.

- The Guru Granth Sahib contains the teaching of human gurus about God's will.

10.8 Birth and initiation

Birth

- **The parents** bring the new **baby** to the **gurdwara**.

- The **baby** is brought to the front of the gurdwara and **held above** the **Guru Granth Sahib**.

- Special **thanksgiving hymns** are sung.

- The **Guru Granth Sahib** is **opened** at **random**.

- The **name** of the child must start with the **first letter** of the **hymn on that page**.

- Sometimes a **kirpan** (sword) is dipped in **amrit** (honey and water) and **touched** on the **baby's tongue**.

- The **Ardas** prayer is said.

- The special **Karah Parshad** food is distributed.

Amritsanskar or initiation

- Initiation occurs around the age of **15**.

- Those wishing to become **Khalsa Sikhs** must show themselves willing to follow the Sikh way of life and wear the five Ks.

- The ceremony is attended by **five Sikhs** who are **full members** of the **Khalsa**.

- They **wear** the **five Ks** and **special saffron coloured robes**.

- The ceremony takes place **privately** in the **gurdwara**.

- The ceremony begins with a **reading** from the **Guru Granth Sahib**.

- Those being **initiated** are asked **various questions**.

- Questions include: 'Do you believe in **one God**?' and 'Will you live by **Sikh teachings**?'.

- **Amrit** is prepared by the **five amrit-dhari** Sikhs with a double-edged **sword**.

- The **candidates** receive the **amrit five times**.

- The **Mul Matra** is said **five times**.

- The **rules** of **Khalsa** are **explained**.

- The **Ardas** is said and there is **a final reading** from the **Guru Granth Sahib**.

- **Some** Sikhs do **not join** the Khalsa but **keep** to its **rules**.

- They are called **kesh-dhari**.

10.9 Gurdwara

- A **Sikh temple** is called a gurdwara.

- **Gurdwara** means **door to the guru**.

- Outside the gurdwara there is usually a **Nishan Sahib** – a **saffron flag** with the symbol of the **Khalsa** on it.

- Sikhs **remove their shoes** and **cover their heads** before entering the gurdwara.

- The **main hall** is called the **diwan** and contains many **pictures** of the **gurus**.

- The **Guru Granth Sahib** is usually placed on a **stool** or **manji** on the **palki** (a **raised platform** with a **canopy**).

- The whole of this **area** is called the **takht** or **throne**.

- The **Guru Granth Sahib** is **protected** by a **person waving** a **fan** or **chauri**.

- **Another room** is set aside for the **Guru Granth Sahib** to be kept in at **night time**.

- Other rooms are for meetings, library, schoolrooms etc.

Worship or diwan in the gurdwara

- **Worshippers** approach the **takht** and make an **offering**.

- Everyone **sits** on the floor with **crossed legs**.

- **Diwan** consists of **hymns** or **kirtan** sung by the **ragis** (singers).

- Everyone **meditates** on the **name of God**.

- There may be **talks** on the **teachings** of the **gurus**.

- The **holy sweet** or **Karah Parshad** is placed **near** the **Guru Granth Sahib**.

- **Karah Parshad** is made from **sugar**, **butter** and **semolina**.

- At the **end** of the service the **Japji** is said.

- Everyone **faces** the **Guru Granth Sahib** for a final **reading**.

- The **final prayer** asks **God to accept** the **Karah Parshad**.

- Everyone is **given** some of the **Karah Parshad**.

The langar or free kitchen

- The **langar** was first **established** by **Guru Nanak**.

- It makes sure people from **different backgrounds eat together**.

- It is a sign of **equality**.

- The **food** is always the **same** for everyone.

- Those who **prepare** the food learn about **service to others**.

- The food is usually **vegetarian**.

- It is a custom for **families** to **take** it **in turns** to buy and prepare the food.

10.10 Festivals

There are many Sikh festivals, but you are only expected to know the following two:

Vaisakhi

- **Vaisakhi** is the **most important** festival.

- It commemorates the **foundation** of the **Khalsa**.

- It is also the **Sikh new year**.

- **Unity**, **courage** and **strength** are celebrated.

- Many individual and team **games** are played.

Diwali

- **Diwali** is celebrated by **Hindus** (but for different reasons) as well as by Sikhs.

- It remembers when **Guru Amar Das** told Sikhs to **gather together**.

- It also remembers when **Guru Hargobind** was **released** from **prison**.

- The story tells how the **emperor allowed** all those who held on to **Guru Hargobind's coat** to be **freed** as well.

- **Kirtan** (singing from the Guru Granth Sahib) takes place in the **gurdwara**.

- **Fireworks** and the lighting of **lamps** celebrate Guru Hargobind's release.

10.11 Marriage and death

Marriage

- The gurus taught that families were particularly important, so Sikhs are strongly encouraged to marry.

- Marriages are **often arranged** but cannot take place unless both bride and groom agree to marry.

- At a **betrothal ceremony** the **girl's family** offer a **kirpan** and **sweets** as a sign of **commitment**.

- Before the ceremony **gifts are exchanged** between the families.

- The ceremony can take place in the **bride's home** or at a **gurdwara**.

- The **Guru Granth Sahib** must be **present**.

- The **bride** and **groom sit facing** the **takht**.

- The **groom** wears a **scarf of red and gold**.

- They are **told** about their **responsibilities**.

- A **blessing** is said for **them** and their **parents**.

- The couple **bow** to the **Guru Granth Sahib** as a sign of **agreement**.

- **Garlands of flowers** are given to them by the **groom's father**.

- The **groom's father** places the **groom's scarf** in the **bride's hands**.

- The **marriage hymn** by **Guru Ram Das** is **read**.

- The couple **circle** round the **Guru Granth Sahib four times**.

- **Flower petals** are **sprinkled** over the **couple**.

- **Sweets** are given to them by the **bride's parents**.

- **Money** is placed in the couple's laps by **guests**.

- Everyone joins in a **meal**.

Death and funerals

- Sikhs regard death as the result of God's will.

- If possible the **gurbani** should be **recited whilst** someone is **dying**.

- When someone has **died** the body is **washed** and dressed in **clean clothes**.

- If the person is a **Khalsa Sikh** then the **five Ks** are worn.

- Last respects are paid by going to a **service** in the **gurdwara**.

- The body is taken to be **cremated**.

- As the body is being taken to the crematorium **hymns are sung** from the Guru Granth Sahib.

- The **Ardas** is said.

- The body is put on the funeral **pyre**.

- **Evening prayer** is recited.

- The **ashes** can be placed in **flowing water** or **buried**.

- **Mourning** can last up to **ten days**.

- A funeral is a time for praising God as much as celebrating the life of the deceased.

10.12 Places of pilgrimage

Pilgrimage is the act of making a journey to a place which has special religious significance. People who make these journeys are known as **pilgrims**.

The Five Takhts

- **Takht** means **throne**.

- The **Five Takhts** are **places** with **spiritual authority** where **religious decisions** are made.

- **Guidance** is offered under the **leaders** of the takhts and the **Guru Granth Sahib**.

- The **chief takht** is **Amritsar** the Akal Takht.

- Other takhts are: **Anandpur**, **Nanded**, **Patna** and **Talwandi Sabo**.

Harimandir, The Golden Temple at Amritsar

- The **Golden Temple** was founded in the **Punjab** in **1589**.

- It has a large **pool for bathing** and a **temple**.

- The **temple** is **highly decorated**.

- **Worshippers** have to **step down** into the temple as a sign of **humility**.

- There is a lot of **black and white marble** and **precious stones**.

- The **walls** are decorated with many **writings from scriptures**.

- The **ground floor** contains the **takht**, **palki** and a **rail to guide worshippers** round the Guru Granth Sahib.

- The **upper floor** is for **reading** of the Guru Granth Sahib.

- There is a **hall of mirrors** to make the place more **beautiful**.

- The **golden dome** gives the temple its **name**.

Summary

You should now know the following:

1. The key moments in the life of Guru Nanak

2. The key moments in the life of Guru Angad

3. The key moments in the life of Guru Gobind Rai

4. What happened at Vaisakhi in **1699 CE** and its importance for Sikhism

5. The significance of the Khalsa

6. The importance of the Rahit Maryada for everyday Sikh life

7. The central Sikh beliefs

8. The key beliefs and ceremonies of birth and initiation

9. The layout and use of the gurdwara

10. The main Sikh festivals

11. The key beliefs and ceremonies of marriage and death

12. The various places of Sikh pilgrimage

Test yourself

Before moving on, make sure you can answer the following questions. Sample answers are given on page 203.

1. Outline the life of Guru Gobind Rai and the first Vaisakhi. (6)

2. Explain the main teachings of the Rahit Maryada. (6)

3. Explain what Sikhs believe by reincarnation. (6)

4. Describe a typical gurdwara. (6)

5. Describe the Harimandir (The Golden Temple at Amritsar). (6)

Test yourself answers

Marks for each question are given in brackets.

Chapter 2: Interpreting the Old Testament

1. The Second Creation story

(a) Adam was punished by having to work and Eve was punished by having childbirth made painful. **(2)**

(b) The Garden of Eden was perfect. In it were two trees, the Tree of Knowledge and the Tree of Life. Adam and Eve were not allowed to eat the fruit. If they did they would be able to know good and evil. In the garden Adam and Eve lived peacefully with the other animals. One of these animals was a serpent. **(6)**

(c) This story teaches that humans have a duty to look after the natural world. Everything has its special place and God gave us the responsibility of making sure that harmony is maintained. This means making sure that animals are respected and humans do not use their power to damage the natural environment but to look after it. Because humans share in God's love they should love the world as He does. **(6)**

(d) Some argue that as God gave us free will, then we must be responsible for our actions. For example, if our parents give us some money to spend, then we are free to use it as we wish but if we buy something which is dangerous or harmful to someone else, then we know that we should take the blame.

On the other hand some people think that as we are naturally selfish and rebellious we cannot be totally responsible for our own actions. For example, some people just get very angry for no reason. In the world there are constant wars and people suffer because governments are corrupt. This definitely seems to support the view in the Bible, as in the story of Cain and Abel, that we do not seem to have complete control over our desires.

Therefore I agree with the statement. I do not think we are always responsible for our own actions. **(7)**

2. The Ten Commandments

(a) Sinai is the Mountain of God. **(2)**

(b) Moses was told that we should have no other gods; that we should keep the Sabbath day holy by working six days and resting on the seventh; that we should honour our father and mother; that we should not murder and steal. **(6)**

(c) First of all the commandments teach that the Israelites should be an example or a light to the world. This means keeping to a very high standard of moral goodness. For example, the commandments mean that when you make a promise you should keep to it. This is important so that we trust each other. They also teach that, as our lives are God-given, we should respect other people and their property. It is also wrong to murder because life is not ours but is given by God. **(6)**

(d) Some people think that the purpose of punishment is not to make people suffer but to make them change their attitudes. Being punished means that if you can feel some of the hurt which you have caused someone else to feel, you might then be sorry for what you have done. This is what Jesus wanted people to do when he asked them to repent and change their ways.

On the other hand others think that reform is not enough. It does not really make the victim feel any better and punishment is making someone suffer by having things taken away from them and making them experience how angry other people are with them. Therefore if they have done something really bad, such as murder, then they should be killed.

I do not think we should deliberately make a wrongdoer suffer, because this would be an eye for an eye and two wrongs do not make a right. **(7)**

3. David and Bathsheba

(a) Temptation is the desire to do something wrong. **(2)**

(b) King David saw Bathsheba, the wife of Uriah the Hittite, bathing on her roof. David had sex with her and then set about trying to get rid of Uriah so he could marry Bathsheba. First he brought Uriah home to report on the war. He thought if he could do this then Uriah would sleep with Bathsheba and then he would think that she was having his child. But Uriah would not leave his men. David tried to get Uriah drunk but eventually he sent him to the front line where he was killed. Now he could marry Bathsheba. **(6)**

(c) The story does not show David in a very good light. First he was driven by lust not reason. He used his power to have sex with another man's wife. This is adultery and, as David was supposed to be the 'shepherd of his people', this makes him a hypocrite. Then he misuses his power through cunning and lying by trying to get Uriah to think Bathsheba is having his baby. Finally it shows how cruel David is by having Uriah deliberately killed in battle. **(6)**

(d) Some think that the more power and authority a person has, the more they should to be expected to be punished if they misuse their power. This is because power brings lots of privileges – more money, a bigger house, a great social life. As we see in Nathan's parable, the more someone has, the more responsible they have to be with it. It is only fair for them to be punished more as they have had greater advantages.

On the other hand, the law should treat everyone the same. For example, whether one is Harold Shipman, who misused his responsibility as a doctor to kill many of his patients, or a thug who kills another person in a fight, they have both killed and both should be treated equally under the law.

However, I agree that it is only fair to punish someone more who has misused their authority because they should know better. **(7)**

4. Isaiah's message

(a) A prophet is a person chosen by God to speak God's message to the people. **(2)**

(b) Isaiah says that the leaders and people of Judah have become corrupt and failed to listen to God's law. For example, although they carry out sacrifices and say the right words of the prayers, in their hearts they aren't really worshipping God. Their worship is meaningless. Isaiah says their hands are full of blood and therefore God will judge them by destroying them. **(6)**

(c) Isaiah says Judah is so badly sinful because the people have rejected God's love. As God's children they are supposed to show God love, respect and obedience, but they only pretend to love God and use the festivals just to enjoy themselves. That is why all their religion is meaningless. The heart of the problem is that they have not carried out the most basic duties of the law. They have not protected the weak and the marginalised, and they have not practised justice. All they have shown God is lip service not worship from the heart. **(6)**

(d) Isaiah's message was very harsh because the leaders and people of Judah were still carrying out some of their religious duties by keeping festivals and offering sacrifices. It could have been a great deal worse. They could have rejected God altogether and started to worship the gods of the Assyrians or Egyptians. Finally, Isaiah is writing during some difficult political times. It must have been hard for the people to worship God when at any time they could have been destroyed by the Assyrians.

On the other hand, Isaiah says that, although the people's sins are like scarlet, they can still repent and God will make them pure. In other words Isaiah's message was one of hope that the special relationship God has with His people can be repaired.

I do not think Isaiah's message was too harsh. After all we all value justice, and Isaiah was right to use strong language to make the leaders and people of Judah realise quite how corrupt they had become. **(7)**

Chapter 3: Interpreting the New Testament

1. The rich young man

(a) Sacrifice means giving up something for something else of greater value. **(2)**

(b) A rich man came up to Jesus and asked him what he should do to inherit eternal life. Jesus told him he should keep the Ten Commandments. The man said he had kept to all these since he was a child. Jesus set him a further challenge. He told the man that he should now sell everything and give the money to the poor. The man went away very sad because he was unable to do this. **(6)**

(c) In Jesus' time having great wealth was a sign that a person had been blessed by God. So the man's question to Jesus was really asking Jesus to confirm that he was a good person. He wanted Jesus to praise him. But Jesus' challenge was to test whether the man really understood what justice meant and to reverse the usual ideas in society and look after the weak and the poor. Looking after the poor is a sign of true discipleship. But the rich man cannot be a disciple because he is thinking only about himself. **(6)**

(d) Having great wealth is not good because it often means a person is more interested in getting money than being really concerned for others. That is why Jesus said that it was easier for a camel to pass through an eye of a needle than for a rich man to enter the Kingdom of God. Mother Teresa is a good example of someone who dedicated her life to the poor because she knew that this would bring her greater happiness than being very rich.

On the other hand, having great wealth is a chance to use money wisely for others. If there weren't rich people in the world there would be nobody to give money to people like Mother Teresa who worked to help the poor.

I think that people should have wealth, but I do not think *great* wealth is good because it does not usually make people happy. **(7)**

2. The Parable of the Sower

(a) A parable is a story or saying comparing the Kingdom of God with everyday human events. **(2)**

(b) A sower went out to sow the seed on his field. Some seed fell on the path and was eaten by birds. Some seed fell on rocky ground and grew for a while and then died from lack of moisture. Some fell amongst the thorns and grew but then was choked by them. Some fell on good ground and produced a hundred per cent more than was sown. **(6)**

(c) Jesus told parables to explain in everyday terms his teaching about the Kingdom of God. The Kingdom of God is about God's special relationship with us. This parable is about how different people react to Jesus' teaching about the Kingdom. Some reject it without ever listening to it. Others listen for a while but do not make a real effort to meet its challenge, and others like the idea but prefer their money and wealth. The parable is to encourage the disciples to keep going, because many will listen and the spiritual rewards are great. **(6)**

(d) This is a very sweeping statement but it is true that many people do not really think deeply about what they believe is important. Some are happy just to get on with life, doing the shopping, going to the football match, watching tv and having a good time, just as Jesus taught in the Parable of the Sower. Not a huge number of people go to church and many people are not interested in politics as they do not vote.

On the other hand, most of the population say they believe in God and more people in the world belong to a religion than do not. When people die or there is suffering in the family, then people often express their beliefs clearly.

I think all people have beliefs, but as these are often quite private it is difficult to know whether they hold them strongly or not. **(7)**

3. Peter's declaration

(a) Son of Man refers to Jesus' role as the one who would suffer for others. **(2)**

(b) On the road to Caesarea Philippi Jesus asked the disciples who the people they were preaching to thought he was. They answered that some thought he was John the Baptist, some thought he was Elijah or a prophet. Jesus asked his disciples who they thought he was. Peter answered that Jesus was the Messiah. Then Jesus told them that the Son of Man would suffer many things and then be killed. **(6)**

(c) When Jesus explained that he would suffer as a Messiah he probably knew that this was not what the disciples thought the Messiah should be. They all imagined that the Messiah would bring a time of peace, compassion and justice. Jesus' healings and treatment of the outcasts show that this is his aim. But Peter's words show that he cannot understand how Jesus' suffering will achieve these things. Jesus' idea is that the Messiah must suffer for others. **(6)**

(d) Some might argue that Jesus must have been more than a good man because good people do not usually have the power to cure the sick and even bring people back to life again, as he did to Jairus' daughter. That is why for Christians he is the Son of God. His resurrection is proof of this.

On the other hand, there is no proof that the Resurrection took place and it may just be a story to explain how Jesus' message inspired his disciples after his death. But Jesus did do a lot of good and he challenged people to be loving and kind to each other.

I agree that Jesus was no more than a good man because it is difficult to know what the Resurrection means but his life is a very good example of someone who was prepared to die for what he believed in. **(7)**

4. Jesus' resurrection

(a) Son of God refers to Jesus' unique relationship with God. **(2)**

(b) Thomas complained that he had not met the risen Jesus and he said unless he had seen him and touched the wounds on Jesus' hands and side he would not believe. A few days later when the disciples were meeting, even though the doors were locked, Jesus appeared and told Thomas to touch his hands and side. Thomas did so and said 'My Lord and my God'. Jesus told him those who were blessed were those who believe without seeing. **(6)**

(c) The story teaches that sometimes physical proof or evidence is necessary in order to believe. Thomas needed to touch Jesus' hands and side and to experience the marks of the Crucifixion. Jesus does not say this is wrong. Some people need to experience miracles or feel their prayers are answered in order to believe in God.

However, Jesus also praises those who believe without the need of evidence. He calls them blessed because they have to work on a higher level of trust. Perhaps they have only the Bible to read or the teachings of the Church and from this they have to make a leap of faith. Thomas is told that it is a superior form of belief. **(6)**

(d) If a person doubts their beliefs then they cannot really be said to have those beliefs in the first place. A religious person in particular should have no doubts, because Jesus is no longer around to see and touch and so belief has to be something you think about and then make a commitment. This is what happens when a person is confirmed. First they have courses to discuss Christian beliefs and then at the end they say they believe them – that is what makes them a Christian.

On the other hand, doubting does not mean a person does not believe. I might doubt something in order to make the idea clearer, or to get rid of confusions. After all, religious beliefs aren't always easy and doubt is a way of coming to understand them deeply.

I think doubt is important for religious belief, so I disagree with the statement. I also think that a person who has no doubt cannot develop their ideas and this might make it very difficult for them to adapt to new situations. **(7)**

Chapter 4: Contemporary issues

1. Creationists are Christians who believe that the Bible was directly inspired by the Holy Spirit. Therefore the Bible has greater authority than science and offers a more accurate view of how the world was made than cosmologists do. Creationists reject Darwinism because God created humans specially as Genesis describes and they did not evolve from lower life forms as evolutionists claim. **(6)**

2. Christian stewardship means looking after the planet as God commanded in Genesis 1. Being a steward means acting on God's behalf and repairing all the bad things humans have done to the environment. Stewardship is based on the covenant with God and might include conservation and treating animals with care. **(6)**

3. According to the United Nation's Convention on the Rights of the Child, children need special rights because they are vulnerable and need special protection. They have rights to a stable family and to be protected from harm and abuse. They have a right to education. Jesus supported children's rights because he believed that we should always protect the weaker members of society. **(6)**

4. Bonhoeffer was a Christian minister and academic. When Hitler came to power he was lecturing on Christian ethics in America. He realised that many citizens in

Germany were suffering because they were resisting the Nazis and his conscience told him that he could not be a good Christian unless he went home to help. He became part of the Confessing Church and was executed by the Nazis. **(6)**

5. The Christian teaching on the sanctity of life states that, as God made humans in his own image, they are special and their lives must be treated with respect. Life is therefore a gift from God and only God can take it away. This is why the Ten Commandments say it is wrong to kill. Life is considered sacred by many Christians from the moment of conception according to Psalm 139. **(6)**

Chapter 5: Christianity

1. Jesus was born in Bethlehem to Mary and Joseph. We do not know much about his early life, but when he was 30 he was baptised by John the Baptist and started to preach in Galilee. His teaching upset the leaders of Judaism. His friend Judas betrayed him to the Jewish authorities who handed him over to the Romans. Pilate had Jesus crucified. But three days later Jesus rose from the dead and later ascended to heaven. **(6)**

2. Most Christians marry in a church. The service begins when the minister explains the purpose of marriage and then the bride and bridegroom make their promises to each other. They promise to love, honour and obey each other for the rest of their lives. Then they may exchange rings and the minister says they have now become husband and wife. **(6)**

3. The Bible is important for Christians because it is believed to be the word of God. That means it is not like any other book but was inspired by the Holy Spirit and can therefore guide Christians in their daily lives. Many Christians study the Bible in groups or listen to it being read in church as part of their worship of God. **(6)**

4. Christians believe that there is only one God who created everything. But they also believe that he exists as the Trinity. As Father He creates everything, as Son He became human in the person of Jesus Christ and as Holy Spirit He is everywhere. It is as the Holy Spirit that God is able to be a source of inspiration for Christians today. **(6)**

5. Christians often go on pilgrimage to the Holy Land (modern Israel). They may visit Bethlehem where Jesus was born and go to the Church of the Nativity. Some travel to Galilee where Jesus spent most of his life and to Capernaum where he taught. Most importantly pilgrims go to Jerusalem and follow the road which Jesus took on his way to his crucifixion. This road is called the Via Dolorosa. **(6)**

Chapter 6: Judaism

1. For Orthodox Jews a body should be buried as soon after the person has died as possible. The body is prepared and dressed in a white garment. After the body is buried everyone washes their hands in a special ceremony. It is usual for the bereaved family to stay at home for a week and for people to visit them. Men do not shave and women do not wear make-up. The kaddish prayer is said in the synagogue. **(6)**

2. The Shabbat begins at sunset when the mother of the family lights two candles and says a special blessing. During the day she will have prepared the house and her husband and sons may have attended the synagogue. When he returns the father says kiddush over the wine and a blessing over the special challah bread. After eating the bread and wine the family eat the Shabbat meal and at the end sing Jewish songs. **(6)**

3. The Torah is the first five books of the Hebrew Bible, the 613 commandments needed for Jews to live good lives. Jews also believe that Moses was given the Oral Torah, that is all the other laws and teachings needed to keep the written Torah. This is in the Talmud. Talmud means to study. **(6)**

4. Jews believe in two ages – the present age and a world to come where there will be no violence, everyone will live in peace with one another and there will be justice for everyone for ever. They believe that the Messiah will come first and prepare the world for its coming. Some believe that the world to come could be the afterlife in heaven. **(6)**

5. Sukkot is an autumn festival which remembers the time when the Israelites were wandering in the wilderness and living in tents. Today Jews build a tent or sukkah and decorate it with fruits. If it is warm enough they live in it during the eight days of the festival. At the synagogue service people hold bundles of willow, palm and myrtle and carry a citron which is waved in the four directions of the world. **(6)**

Chapter 7: Islam

1. Muhammad had been meditating in a cave on Mount Hira outside Makkah when suddenly the angel Gabriel appeared and told him to read. Muhammad said he could not read but the angel squeezed him. This happened two more times and on the third time Muhammad was able to recite God's words. This left him greatly shocked but he was encouraged by his wife Khadijah that it was God who had spoken to him. **(6)**

2. Muslims believe that the Qur'an is God's final revelation to the world given directly to Muhammad over a period of 23 years. It cannot really be translated and should be read in Arabic. Many people learn it by heart. The Hadith are various books which contain the words and actions of Muhammad and are consulted to see how Muhammad understood the Qur'an. **(6)**

3. Muslims believe that angels are God's messengers. They cannot usually be seen and are made of light. They can take on human form, just as Gabriel did when he brought the Qur'an to Muhammad. Everyone has at least one guardian angel who looks after you when you pray. They can be felt as a presence of love and peace. **(6)**

4. When a Muslim arrives in Makkah he changes into simple white clothes to prepare himself for spiritual purity or ihram. There are lots of ceremonies to carry out. The important ones are circling the Ka'bah seven times and running between the two hills and the Zamzam well. After camping he stands in the Plain of Arafat and prays to God. Then he throws stones at the pillars of Mina to drive out Satan before returning to Makkah. **(6)**

5. It is expected in Islam that men and women will marry. Sex should only occur in marriage. They should both dress modestly and set a good example to their children. This means that husbands and wives should respect their parents and educate and feed their children as best as they can. Husbands must provide money for the family and protect their wives. Wives must look after their guests and feed the hungry. **(6)**

Chapter 8: Hinduism

1. The story is about the battle between good and evil and is told as a war between two warring families. The blind eldest Kuru brother could not become king so he let his brother Pandu rule instead. But Pandu wanted to become a holy man, so he gave the kingdom to his brother Dhritavashtra. But Dhritavashtra's sons tried to kill Pandu's sons. Pandu's sons escaped, led by Arjuna. In a great battle the Pandus defeated the Kurus and ruled wisely afterwards. **(6)**

2. Atman means soul. Every living thing has atman and when it dies the atman leaves the body and moves on to another body. This is called samsara. Samsara also describes the process of change we all go through in our lives. For example, my character is not the same now as when I was little, but I am deep down the same person. Atman is also part of Brahman. **(6)**

3. The festival of Holi takes place in spring. It remembers the time when the wicked Princess Holika tried to kill her nephew but was burned in the fire instead. So, at the festival, bonfires are lit. As the festival also remembers Lord Krishna, who liked practical jokes, this is also a time of playing lots of tricks on people. Children are allowed to be cheeky to adults. **(6)**

4. After the bride has prepared herself and put on her best sari the wedding begins and the couple take seven steps round a fire. This symbolises their hope for children and happiness in the presence of God. They also carry a scarf to show how their lives are now joined together. On the final step they are now husband and wife. Sometimes rice grain is sprinkled over the couple. **(6)**

5. Worship in the temple begins when a person enters the building and rings a bell to tell the deity they have arrived. Some people sing hymns or prayers. The priest performs arti by passing around a lamp and the people place their hands near it to come into the presence of God. Worshippers make offerings to the deity of money, food and flowers and in return the priest gives them prashad or special food. **(6)**

Chapter 9: Buddhism

1. Siddartha set out from his palace because he wanted to see what the real world was like. He saw an old person, then a sick person, then a dead person and finally a holy man. This showed him that the world is full of decay and suffering. But the holy man taught him that a life of prayer and meditation might help him to live a contented life. That was what he set off to find. **(6)**

2. The sangha is the worldwide community of all Buddhists. However, it often refers to Buddhist monks and nuns who have special duties. In the sangha all people are equal, but the duty of a monk is to study the Buddha's dharma and to live in a vihara or monastery. Monks and nuns have a duty to teach dharma so they can achieve enlightenment. **(6)**

3. Zen Buddhism teaches that everyone has a Buddha nature. A person can discover their Buddha nature through careful training of the mind and becoming aware of all their actions. This is why flower arranging or tea ceremonies are important.

    In Tibetan Buddhism meditation is important and it is done through special chants or mantras. The Tibetan monks like debates. At festivals there is a lot of dancing and music. **(6)**

4. The images are used to help in meditation. Some images of the Buddha show various moments in his life and are useful to explain how he learnt to live by the middle way. Other images express some of the inner experiences of the Buddha. Some images are of bodhisattvas, or other beings who have become enlightened. All these images can be used in a shrine at home. **(6)**

5. The main teaching is found in the Five Precepts. These teach that a Buddhist should avoid killing deliberately and not take things which do not belong to him. They should not tell lies or have sex which causes harm to others. They should earn their money fairly and avoid working in jobs, such as the army, which involve killing people. They should treat the environment with loving kindness. **(6)**

Chapter 10: Sikhism

1. Guru Gobind Rai was the last of the ten gurus. He was a strong leader and managed to restore the Sikh faith in God. He was famous for training Sikhs to become soldiers and to protect the weak.

   In 1699 at Vaisakhi, Gobind Rai asked for volunteers to give their heads for him. Five volunteered but Gobind Rai did not actually kill them – it was a test of their dedication. This group became the basis of the Khalsa or pure community.   **(6)**

2. The Rahit Maryada is a book setting out how a Sikh should live his life. It teaches that a Sikh is anyone who believes in the one God, the teaching of the ten gurus and baptism by Amrit. It teaches that in the family children must be educated and their hair should not be cut. It teaches that no Sikh should drink or take drugs. It also teaches that Sikhs should do voluntary work in the community.   **(6)**

3. Sikhs believe that if you have not lived an entirely good life and have been selfish and ignored God's will, then you will be reborn to live another life. If however you have listened to the gurbani and meditated on God's name and not been envious of others or greedy, then you receive mukti. Mukti is to be released by God from the cycle of rebirths.   **(6)**

4. Gurdwaras usually have a saffron flag flying outside the temple with the sign of the Khalsa on it. In the main hall or diwan of the temple there are pictures of the great gurus. On the palki the Guru Granth Sahib is placed on a stool or manji. Over the palki is a canopy. There is another room for the Guru Granth Sahib to be kept overnight. Other rooms are for teaching and the preparation of food. **(6)**

5. One of the great sights of the Golden Temple is its large pool for bathing and the golden dome. The temple itself is beautifully decorated with black and white marble and many precious stones. The walls are covered by passages from the Sikh scriptures and there is a hall of mirrors. On the ground floor are the takht and the palki. There is a room upstairs for reading the Guru Granth Sahib.   **(6)**

Guide to coursework

Coursework is an alternative to sitting Section 3 (World Religions and Contemporary Issues) as part of the timed examination.

Coursework is usually marked by the **senior school** in just the same way as the examination papers, and not by teachers of your school.

Coursework must be submitted to the senior school by the end of the second term in the year in which you are taking Common Entrance, i.e. by late March.

If there is any doubt about the coursework title or type of project you want to carry out, you should contact your senior school well in advance.

Coursework should be between **750 and 1500** words, certainly no longer. Often a shorter focussed project will score more highly than one that it is unnecessarily long.

Coursework is a chance for you to show off your academic skills. You can begin with the prescribed textbooks, use the library, interview people and use the internet. However, it is essential that you use your **own words** and avoid copying from books, CD ROMs and the internet. Senior schools will not be impressed if you simply copy material and you will not score high marks.

An aspect of a major world religion or contemporary issue

The syllabus states the following aims for coursework:

> 'Coursework may be offered instead of Section 3, the World Religions and Contemporary Issues section. This option invites candidates to research a particular religious moral belief or practice from one major world religion as examined in Section 3. The research for this might include textbooks, interviews, internet, visiting speakers etc.'

Such studies might include:

- the **key religious leaders** or thinkers

- central **religious beliefs** and their meaning today

- main **religious practices** such as daily/weekly worship, rites of passage (birth, marriage and death) and major festivals

- a particular **moral belief** about a contemporary issue and the religious and non-religious responses to it

- the life of a particular **faith community** (church, synagogue, temple, mosque, etc); its place in the local community; the role of its religious leader(s) .

By far the best approach is to find **one** particular area of a religion on which to do your research. Trying to cover the whole of a religion will result in a very general project which will not show off what you have thought about in your research.

Here are some examples of coursework titles:

- 'The work of Cicely Saunders and the debate about euthanasia'

- 'The religious and non-religious views on racism'

- 'The importance of Jewish life at home'

- 'Why Muslims go on hajj'

- 'The significance of Easter for Christians'

- 'How the Eightfold Path affects everyday life for Buddhists'

- 'What Hindus believe about God'

- 'The key moments from birth to death in Sikhism'

Format of coursework and marks for each part

You should set out your coursework as follows:

- **Introduction and investigative methods** (5 marks). An **introduction** of about 50 words stating the aims of your project and the main areas which you have chosen to investigate; some background information if appropriate; how the information has been obtained.

- **Presentation of the research** (25 marks). The **main areas** of your project should be between 750 and 1200 words (allowing for your introduction and conclusion). Use chapter headings, footnotes (if necessary), maps, pictures, charts etc. Remember that pictures and maps are only to be included when they are relevant and help to clarify the ideas.

- **Conclusion** (4 marks). The conclusion should be no more than 50 words and should summarise briefly what you have found out, its significance and possible areas for future study.

- **Acknowledgements** (2 marks). Make a list of the main books, websites and resources you have used.

The total mark is out of 36 which is then divided by two.

Coursework cover sheet

Make sure you attach the ISEB official coursework cover sheet with your coursework.

- Write your name, present school and senior school for which you are entered on it.

- Sign it to say the work is your own.

- Attach it securely to your coursework.

Appendix 1: Examination paper

This is how a typical examination paper is laid out:

SECTION 1: INTERPRETING THE OLD TESTAMENT

Answer **one** question from this section.

A. God, human nature and covenant

1. The Second Creation story

(a) Name two ways God punished Adam and Eve. (2)

(b) Describe the main features of the Garden of Eden. (6)

(c) Explain what the creation story teaches about human stewardship of the world. (6)

(d) 'We are not always responsible for the consequences of our actions.' Do you agree? Give reasons to support your answer. (7)

2. The Ten Commandments

(a) What is Sinai? (2)

(b) Describe any five of the Ten Commandments. (6)

(c) Explain what this story teaches about the relationship between God and humans. (6)

(d) 'The aim of any punishment is to make the wrongdoer suffer.' Do you agree? Give reasons to support your answer. (7)

B. Leaders and prophets

3. David and Bathsheba

(a) What is temptation? (2)

(b) Describe how David came to marry Bathsheba. (6)

(c) Explain what this story teaches about David as a ruler. (6)

(d) 'Leaders should be punished more than ordinary people if they misuse their authority.' Do you agree? Give reasons to support your answer. (7)

4. Isaiah's message

(a) What is a prophet? (2)

(b) Outline Isaiah's message of judgement against the leaders and people of Judah. (6)

(c) Explain why God does not accept Judah's sacrifices and worship. (6)

(d) 'Isaiah's message was too harsh.' Do you agree? Give reasons to support your answer. (7)

(Total marks for this section: 21)

SECTION 2: INTERPRETING THE NEW TESTAMENT

Answer **one** question from this section.

A. Jesus' teaching

1. The rich young man

(a) What does sacrifice mean? (2)

(b) Outline the story of the rich young man. (6)

(c) Explain what this story teaches about wealth and discipleship. (6)

(d) 'No one should have great wealth.' Do you agree? Give reasons to support your answer. (7)

2. The Parable of the Sower

(a) What is the meaning of the term parable? (2)

(b) Outline the Parable of the Sower. (6)

(c) Explain why Jesus told this parable. (6)

(d) 'Most people do not have strong beliefs.' Do you agree? Give reasons to support your answer. (7)

B. Jesus' life, death and resurrection

3. Peter's declaration

(a) What does the title Son of Man mean? (2)

(b) Describe the conversation between Jesus and his disciples at Caesarea Philippi. (6)

(c) Explain what this event teaches about Jesus' role as the Messiah. (6)

(d) 'Jesus was no more than just a good man.' Do you agree? Give reasons to support your answer. (7)

4. Jesus' resurrection

(a) What does Son of God mean? (2)

(b) Describe the time when Jesus appeared to Thomas. (6)

(c) Explain what the story of Thomas teaches about belief.   (6)

(d) 'If a person is religious they should have no doubts about their beliefs.'
     Do you agree? Give reasons to support your answer.   (7)

(Total marks for this section: 21)

SECTION 3: WORLD RELIGIONS and CONTEMPORARY ISSUES

Answer **three** questions from this section. You may answer from one or more parts.

Do not answer this section if you have submitted coursework.

A. Contemporary Issues

1. Describe the views of Creationists.   (6)

2. Outline what Christians mean by 'stewardship of the environment'.   (6)

3. Outline the reasons for having children's rights.   (6)

4. Describe how Dietrich Bonhoeffer's leadership was based on conscience.   (6)

5. Outline the Christian teaching on the sanctity of life.   (6)

B. Christianity

6. Describe the main events of Jesus' life.   (6)

7. Describe what happens at a typical Christian wedding ceremony.   (6)

8. Explain why the Bible is important for Christians.   (6)

9. Explain what Christians believe about God.   (6)

10. Describe **one** place where Christians go on pilgrimage.   (6)

C. Judaism

11. Describe what happens at a Jewish funeral.   (6)

12. Describe how Shabbat is celebrated at home.   (6)

13. Describe what Jews believe about the Torah and the Talmud.   (6)

14. Describe what Jews believe about the world to come.   (6)

15. Describe any **one** important Jewish festival.   (6)

D. Islam

16. Describe what happened at Muhammad's call.   (6)

17. Describe what Muslims believe about the Qur'an and Hadith.   (6)

18. Explain what Muslims believe about angels. (6)

19. Describe what happens on hajj (pilgrimage). (6)

20. Describe the roles of men and women in the Muslim family. (6)

E. Hinduism

21. Describe the story in the Mahabharata. (6)

22. Explain the Hindu teaching on atman and samsara (reincarnation). (6)

23. Describe **one** Hindu festival. (6)

24. Describe what happens at a typical Hindu wedding. (6)

25. Describe worship in a Hindu temple. (6)

F. Buddhism

26. Describe Siddhartha's (the Buddha's) quest and the four sights. (6)

27. Explain what is meant by the sangha. (6)

28. Describe briefly any **two** different kinds of Buddhism. (6)

29. Explain Buddhists' use of images in worship. (6)

30. Describe the main teachings on the Buddhist way of life. (6)

G. Sikhism

31. Outline the life of Guru Gobind Rai and the first Vaisakhi. (6)

32. Explain the main teachings of the Rahit Maryada. (6)

33. Explain what Sikhs believe by reincarnation. (6)

34. Describe a typical gurdwara. (6)

35. Describe the Harimandir (The Golden Temple at Amritsar). (6)

(Total marks for this section: 18)

Appendix 2: Levels of response

Your answers will be examined according to the following levels of response. It is worth looking at these carefully so you know what to aim for.

AO1: Knowledge

Sections 1 and 2 (question a)

Level	Mark	Level Descriptor
1–2	1	Gives one simple piece of relevant information.
3–4	2	Gives two correct and appropriately detailed pieces of knowledge.

AO1: Knowledge

Sections 1 and 2 (question b), Section 3

Level	Mark	Level Descriptor
1	1	Gives a **very poor** answer: an isolated example of a simple piece of relevant information.
2	2	Gives a **basic** answer: limited knowledge of a relevant idea presented in a structured way.
3	3	Gives a **broadly satisfactory** answer: a description presented in a structured way but lacking detail and some knowledge; moderate use of English.
4	4	Gives a **satisfactory** answer: a description showing more detailed knowledge and understanding.
5	5	Gives a **good** answer: a detailed description with a high level of knowledge and understanding.
6	6	Gives a **very good** answer: a coherent and comprehensive description with precision; almost faultless account of the details; very good command of English.

AO2: Understanding

Sections 1 and 2 (question c)

Level	Mark	Level Descriptor
1	1	Gives a **very poor** answer: an isolated example of a simple piece of relevant information.
2	2	Gives a **basic** answer: limited understanding of a relevant idea.

3	3	Gives a **broadly satisfactory** answer: an explanation presented in a structured way but lacking detail and some knowledge; moderate use of English.
4	4	Gives a **satisfactory** answer: explanation of more than one idea presented in with some detail and understanding.
5	5	Gives a **good** answer: a detailed explanation of several ideas with a good level of knowledge and understanding.
6	6	Gives a **very good** answer: a coherent and comprehensive explanation of several ideas (with sound reference to background, history, other relevant passages etc); very good command of English.

AO3: Evaluation

Sections 1 and 2 (question d)

Level	Mark	Level Descriptor
1	1	Gives a **very poor** answer: no essay structure; a very brief answer; a statement with no reasoning; very little reference to the question; poor or irrelevant examples; makes little sense.
2	2	Gives a **basic** answer: a viewpoint is expressed with minimum justification; an example given; limited relevance.
3	3	Gives a **broadly satisfactory** answer: some structure or organisation of ideas; lacks clear reasoning; some relevant points; unbalanced; limited examples.
4	4	Gives a **satisfactory** answer: reasonably clear structure and balanced answer; some examples and sound explanation; reasonable expression; one or two relevant points made with reasons.
5	5	Gives a **good** answer: good, clear structure and balanced answer; well-chosen examples with a sound grasp of their meaning; sound assessment of ideas with good reasons.
6	6	Gives a **very good** answer: very good structure; ideas developed in a balanced way; insightful reasons / evaluation; well-chosen and relevant examples.
6	7	Gives an **excellent** answer: excellent structure and balanced answer; sharp reasoning; very good use of language; always focuses on the question; uses well-chosen examples to illustrate the points being made.

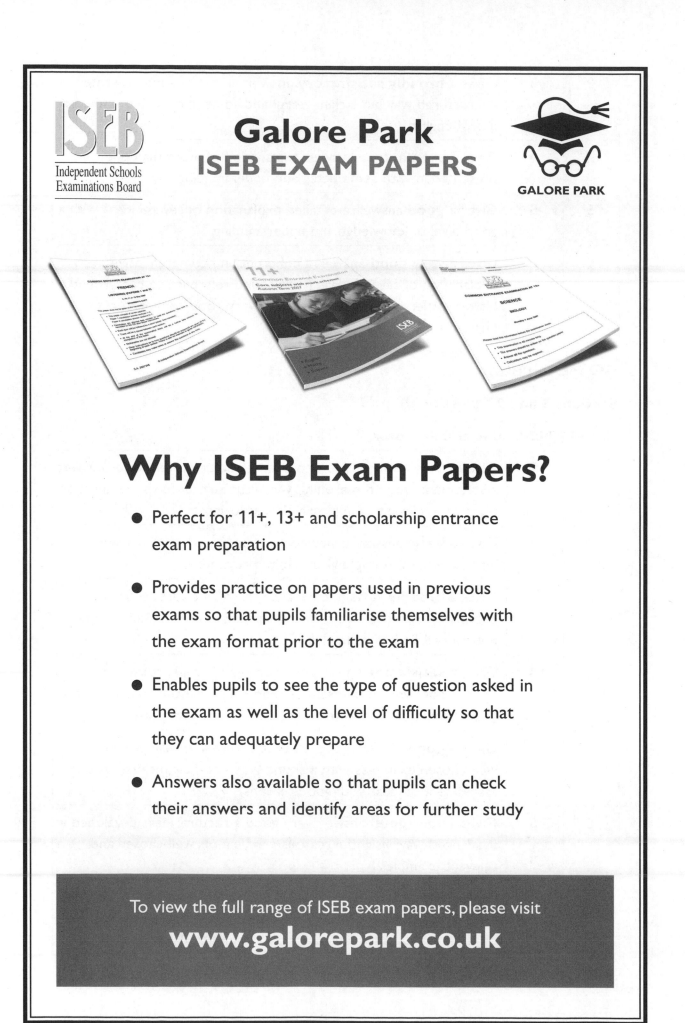

212

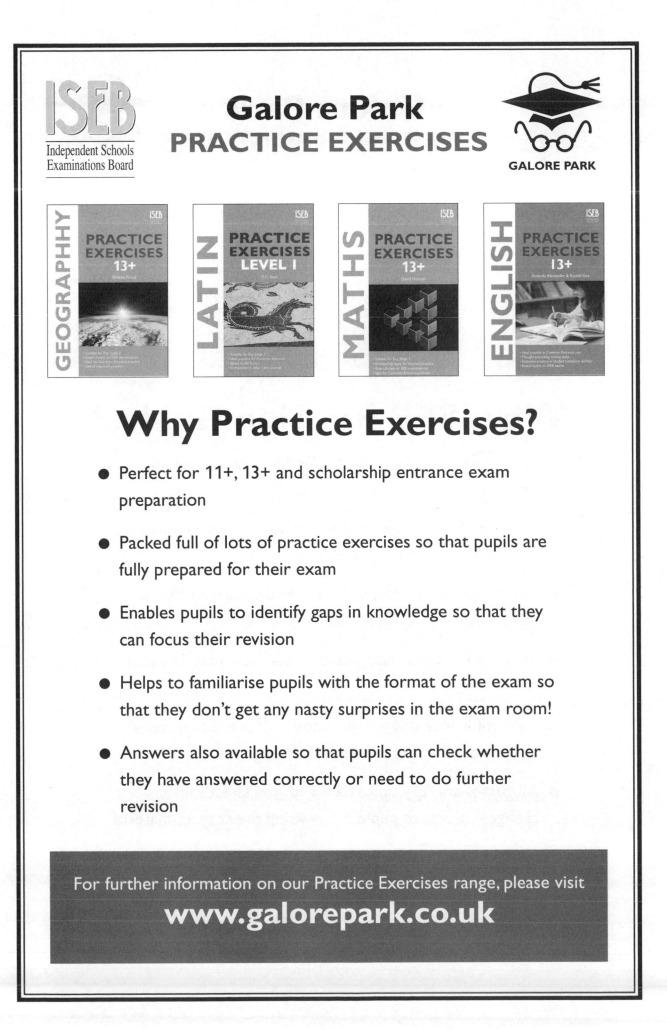

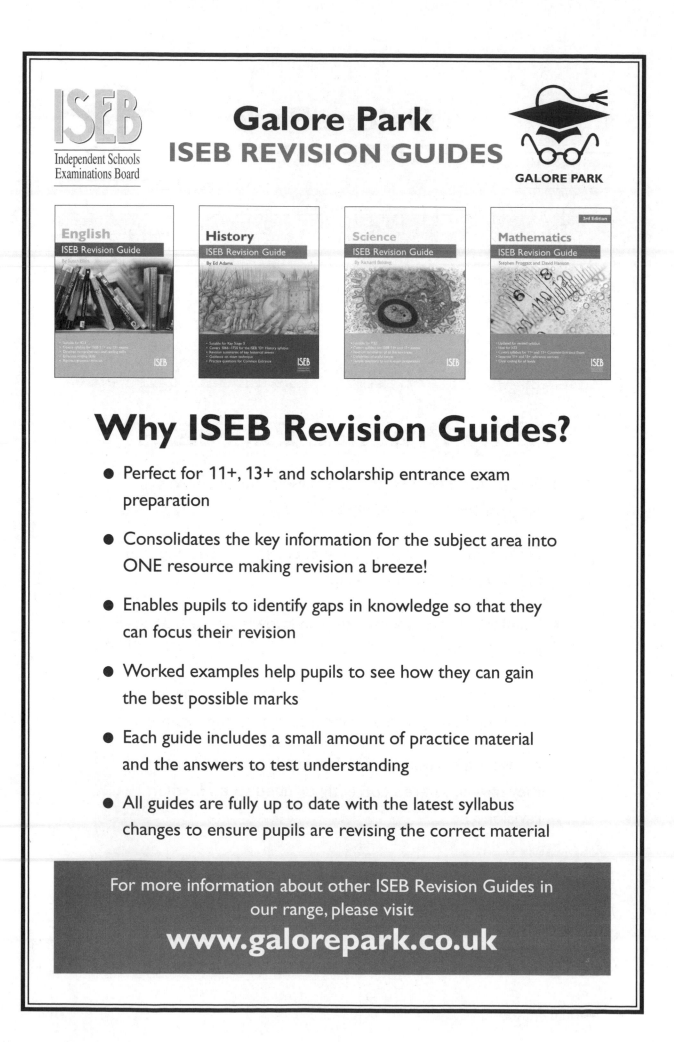

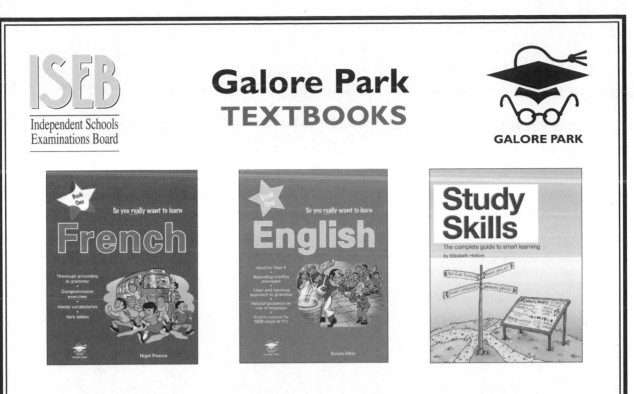